Managing Your Inner Artist / Writer:

Strategies for Success

by M.L. Buchman(s)

Buchman Bookworks

Copyright 2014 Matthew Lieber Buchman
Published by Buchman Bookworks, Inc.
All rights reserved.

This book, or parts thereof,
may not be reproduced in any form
without permission from the author.

Discover more by this author at:
www.buchmanbookworks.com

Cover images:
Hand take white ball with red inscription
Goals achieving ID 77648568 © Emevil
Fine Writing Instrument (back cover)
© Shawn Roberts

Dedication

To our spouses for supporting our Inner Artist
and putting up with our outer mayhem.

> *"Twenty years from now you will be more disappointed by the things that you didn't do than by the ones you did do. So throw off the bowlines. Sail away from the safe harbor. Catch the trade winds in your sails. Explore. Dream. Discover."* –Mark Twain

And a special thanks from brother to sister for stepping outside of your visual art and into mine of words to share your ideas. -Matt

Table of Contents

Section I: The Basics

Chapter 1 – Working with Your Inner Artist – Part I...11

Chapter 2 – Project Defined...23

Chapter 3 – Goals Basics...33

Chapter 4 – Finding Your Big Goal...63

Chapter 5 – What About All Those Other Goals...81

Section II: Taking it Up a Notch

Chapter 6 – Time Management – Part I...99

Chapter 7 – Working with Your Inner Artist – Part II...109

Section III: Making it Practical

Chapter 8 – Time Management – Part II...121

Chapter 9 – Risk Management...135

Chapter 10 – The Action Plan...147

Chapter 11 – Working with Your Inner Artist – Part III...155

Section IV: Taking it "Home" And Owning It

Chapter 12 – Core Principles – why you do what you do...165

Chapter 13 – Project Block...171

Chapter 14 – Working with Your Inner Artist – a few final words...179

Introduction & the Authors

PURPOSE / ORIGINS

The purpose of this work is to lay the groundwork for the artist in each of us to be nurtured. We hope to offer a practical way to allow the business of art to thrive without impinging on the creative process.

This began as a series of lectures presented to both writing and business professionals regarding the project management of an artist, especially when that artist is oneself. It has been presented to hundreds of writers covering every genre.

The authors have collaborated to create a structure and methodology (a way of thinking and a way to do things) that is accessible to every artist whether they are a writer, a photographer, a painter, or a professional sand-sculpturist (who even knew there was such a thing until we saw them specifically disbarred from a local sand-castling competition).

THE AUTHORS

"Why do we have the same initials? Our mother had a good sense of humor."

THE BROTHER—the primary voice of this work
M.L. "Matt" Buchman is an internationally published author of romance, thrillers, and fantasy novels. NPR selected one of his novels as "Top 5 Romance of 2012." Another was picked by Booklist as "Top 10 Romance of 2012." A third was named "Barnes & Noble Best 5 Romance of 2013." He has taught creative fiction writing at the University of Washington as well as lectured at dozens of seminars and conferences over the last twenty years. He has also worked as a project manager for over thirty years and been a trainer on

behalf of Project Management International teaching both new and long-term professionals.

He has led a wide variety of projects in industries as diverse as publishing, law, construction, and I.T. He studied operatic vocal production for several years and has played a wide variety of instruments badly. He had the good sense to fall in love with a research librarian and is the first to proclaim that he has the best kid on the planet (so don't get him started). He is constantly astonished at what can be done with a degree in Geophysics. (http://www.mlbuchman.com)

THE SISTER—the reality check behind this work, because my little brother really needs one!
M.L. "Melitte" Buchman, MFA, a noted practitioner and teacher of tintype photography, has worked for decades leading digital archiving projects for such notable institutions as New York Public Library (NYPL) and New York University (NYU). In frequent demand as a conference speaker, it is the photographic process that motivates her to enter the darkroom and explore what is possible. Her choice

of true love was an abstract painter who worked for decades behind the scenes in various NYC galleries and institutions. Between them, they continue to nurture many artists, especially themselves. (http://www.melittebuchman.com)

WHAT THIS BOOK IS…AND ISN'T

The first lecture in this series began when Matt became overwhelmed by the problems of how to write, work to contract deadlines in traditional publishing, publish his own work in the (then) new indie-publishing, and learn all that he felt he had to learn…while working a totally insane day job.

Through a long series of experiments, both failed and successful, and wide study, we decided that the conflicts and overlaps became easier to manage when we divided our thinking into three areas:

- The craft of our art.
- The business person managing our art.
- The business of our art.

This book is intended to reside completely within the second of these three. This is not a book of craft in any field. Nor is this a book of the business side of whatever craft you practice. This is a book talking to the person who must manage both of these in any field.

Further, within that middle role, we can easily list dozens of sub-roles. These roles can all be filled by one person. (Matt's friend Scott Carter, who we'll revisit later, calls his writing career: "Running a publishing empire from my laptop.") Or these roles can be filled by many people. Each form of art will be unique, but may include common items such as:

- Education
- Educator –for often the best way to learn is to teach
- Finance
- Insurance
- Designer
- Contract specialist
- Materials analyst
- Purchasing
- Marketing…

The list feels infinite, and we have no intention of trying to address infinity (just in case it turns out that the list really is infinite, we'd rather not know). What we are going to focus on is this single, all-important task:

> *Managing your inner artist to the greatest success.*

That success can be defined as monetary, creative, innovative, and a myriad of other ways. But the challenge we faced was: how can we best help that inner artist find their way toward your chosen goal.

This task can't be outsourced. No one can create a document and present it to your inner artist that will help them. No one can demand of the inner artist what they are unable or unwilling to give. Or that they flat out don't understand. Attempting to do so will usually cause anxiety and / or guilt, and shut down the inner artist, the last thing you want.

This role of managing and nurturing *must* be owned by the artist themselves for only they will know what works and what doesn't.

The intention of this book is to offer a tool set to aid "You the practical person" in working in a collaborative (as opposed to authoritative) manner with "You the artist."

LANGUAGE
This book will use the word "Project" frequently. We will explore a variety of definitions, but those are just words. For the purposes of this book, think of a "Project" as whatever it is you create: book, story, photograph, painting, pottery, cupcakes, film, song, cartoons, or any of the thousands of other forms that art takes in our creative lives.

A WORD OF WARNING
We will be presenting dozens of tools and tips for working with your inner artist. Pick them up, try them on, fool around with them, see if they might fit if done a little differently… Whatever works.

HOWEVER! (and we can't emphasize this enough) if you find one of these tools doesn't work for you, don't just put it down. Throw it away! Far away! Fire up the welding torch and make a metal sculpture out of it. None of these are facts, these are ideas and methods and tips, no more, no less.

AND ANOTHER

A few times over the years we have been struck or seen people struck with the "BRILLIANT! MUST CHANGE IT NOW!" idea that will "fix" everything. If this books spurs one of those, great! However, we suggest waiting two weeks.

If it is a truly valid change, it will still be revelatory two weeks from now. If not, the shine will definitely be tarnished within two weeks. We've seen people leap into affairs "Because she understands my art," make extravagant purchases "Because I need that and can't do my art without it," and a dozen other similar messes.

Did we kick off the big brainstorm? Great! Just give it two weeks to make sure that quitting your career, cutting family ties, and moving to Indonesia actually makes sense.

SECTION I
THE BASICS

Chapter 1
Working with Your Inner Artist
Part I

MEET THE ARTIST

There are dozens, and in some fields hundreds of books on: connecting with the inner artist, setting out on a mythic voyage together, cosmic art through deep meditation, how to apply Scrum Master computer programmer scheduling techniques to steer your inner artist down a narrow trail exactly so wide and going exactly in such and such direction. If they work for you, GREAT! Between us we've read many, many of these books, occasionally giving them to each other for Christmas and birthdays (we settled on opposite sides of the U.S., so it's hard to just trade them around). We each use some parts, discard others, often not the same parts.

In almost every book we find a common flaw, or at least a common element. That is:

> *We need to somehow control the inner artist.*

Matt is working on a contracted book right now with a major publisher for his fifth novel in a series. The reason he is drafting this chapter on this day is that his inner artist had a great time doing the first two-thirds of the novel, and then Matt made the mistake of thinking this would get him way ahead of contract especially if the artist would just hurry up on the last third. The artist dug his heels in and here Matt is writing this chapter instead.

So many books talk about fooling "yourself" or convincing "yourself" or buckling down and doing "your work." What we find is that the inner artist is a squirrelly and savvy little dude or gal that thinks in their own way and really, really hates it when someone tries to clamp down on it.

Hence, we have a suggestion. Start with:

WHO IS THE ARTIST ANYWAY?

There are actually a number of studies in psychology to support the idea below. (And no, we're not going into them here. This isn't that sort of book. If you want to study psychology, go for it.)

Imagine a creative genius, ideas pouring forth at a mile-a-minute, who hates being told what to do. Anyone who's had a two-year-old kid, you know exactly what we're talking about. That's your artist. That's the keeper of story.

And we're convinced that almost all art is story. Whether it is the tale telling of a writer, the evocative image of the photographer, or the shout of the graffiti artist; there is a story there to be told and felt. This "creative genius within" is grouchy, elusive, can flip from pure creativity to pure stubbornness way faster than you can blink.

The secret is, it can also flip back the other way and run around the room giggling. As a matter of fact, that's its natural state. So we M.L. Buchman(s) are working every day to "free the inner artist" just as so many of those artist self-help books would have us do.

One of our keys? Split-brain thinking.

SPLIT-BRAIN THINKING

We would suggest that you are not one person, but two. One is the artist and one is the person who "lives in the real world." There is a part of every artist who *wants* to live in the real world. When someone tells us to do that, there is a part of us that wants to achieve, that gets high on getting things done. And, most of all, wants success, however we may choose to define success (more on that later).

However, telling the inner artist to "live in the real world" is a sure-fire way to piss them off. If you insist, or even push too hard as Matt did this morning on his artist, you can actually get blocked. Writer's block, more aptly called Project Block, can come from several sources (which we'll address in a later chapter), but the most common source is probably poor communication with yourself.

Hereafter we'll be referring to two people: practical-self and artist-self. (We'll leave it to you to figure out which is which.)

The problem isn't what is being communicated, and possibly not even how you're communicating it, it's who you're communicating it to. Just try telling:

- the inner artist-self to "get their act together"
  or
- the real-world practical-self to "write the next scene."

You will completely stymie both of them, neither one will even know what you mean. Both messages are critical, but they are being delivered to completely the wrong aspects of you.

Our suggestion? Split your brain. Think about who you are communicating with and address that person.

What if instead we said:

- hey, inner artist-self, wanna go play in creative world for a bit?

or

- hey, real-world practical-self, could you make some time in your schedule for the inner artist-self to go play?

These will be much more effective communications.

HINT: Some people even address their artist-self by a different name. We don't because it's still us in there. But if that works for you, may we suggest Lucinda or Clyde. No particular reason, we just like the names.

The big key here is keep your business-person practical-self out of your playspace. The playspace is the giant room filled with just the neatest stuff on the planet. The workplace is a nasty, dark, evil quagmire that your artist-self wants nothing to do with under any circumstances.

KEEPING YOUR "REAL" WORLD
OUT OF THE PLAYSPACE

Why go to the trouble of identifying your creative playspace?

Once you acknowledge the existence of such a distinction, then it becomes easier to separate tasks and make choices. It can even increase your creative productivity. How? For example, Matt works in "sessions" (more on this later). During those sessions, no business is allowed in, *verbotten*. It is strictly creative time. That allows a mental freedom to write without having to worry about other tasks. The artist-self is told, "This is your time. No tricks, honest. Go forth and revel."

Studies have shown that a single interruption of computer programmers will cause them to take eleven minutes to get back up to speed. And that's switching back to the same task as before, never mind a different task. (Having worked as both a programmer and a writer, Matt knows that programming is actually a highly creative space to work in.)

Ever wonder why most corporate computer departments don't have phones that can reach programmers? The Help Desk isn't there so much for the user's convenience, but more to protect the programmers. A programmer is a very expensive resource and corporations want to keep them functioning as efficiently as possible.

Your artist is your most expensive resource. You have spent years, perhaps even decades, feeding their dream, teaching them craft, imbuing yourself with their passion to achieve. They are your most trained and valuable asset. They are the one creating what you will eventually sell, share, display, or even just admire. Your job is to keep out of their way.

Allowing interruptions to your creative time and your creative place can cause:

- Loss of productivity.
- Loss of continuity.
- Loss of joy.

None of these effects are going to get you where you want to go, but so many people allow constant interruptions to distract their inner-artist (can you say social media and e-mail). Let us just say:

"Cut it out!"

Easier said than done? Well, that's why you're reading this book.

BROTHER'S EXPERIENCE
I see my writing time as a place I can go that story overflows. There are tales there that will challenge me, amuse me, infuriate me, and make me cry. Just three days ago, that same writer who kicked me off the keyboard this morning, actually made me weep as I wrote, blinking hard, tears running down my face. My wife said the best part of her day is when she sometimes walks by my office and can hear me chuckling to myself. I had no idea that I was. Story is the infinite playroom where I can take interesting characters, cool research, high emotions, and run them all together to discover what happens.

SISTER'S EXPERIENCE
When I step into the studio I leave behind every part of my daily grind. I don't worry about unwashed dishes, the dog, email from work, the bills. All of that

is strictly left at the door. (!Cell phone off!) Instead I bring with me an idea that's been rattling around in the back of my mind, or I pull out images that inspire me, or I bring in some object that I like the look of.

For my process I try to get to the place of free-association without any particular expectation of what will come next—that is, I try to get my thinking-mind out of the way.

Why would I do something crazy like that? Because it connects me to a broader view, a less preconceived way of looking at things and for some odd reason that makes me happy. For me this is a left brain / right brain kind of thing. Jill Bolte Taylor, describing her "for real" stroke, wrote eloquently about the euphoria of the intuitive. So maybe a lot of us have brains that are made this way. (Highly recommended viewing: http://www.ted.com/talks/jill_bolte_taylor_s_powerful_stroke_of_insight.html or just go to http://www.ted.com and click "Most Viewed.")

YOUR EXPERIENCE
Take a moment to write down or draw or paint what your playspace is. What is the room, space, wilderness…that you play in? Is it clearly defined? Is it a place of infinite possibilities that can include faeries and space ships and Black Hawk helicopters? Does it have rules?

Be very cautious of applying rules to it.

We believe that a project may have rules, but the creative area shouldn't. In writing a military romantic suspense set in the current day real world, that project has rules, not the least of which is a riveting love story. But to restrict that playspace so that the next project can't be how St. Peter hacked his way out of Purgatory so God put him in charge of security for the Gates of Heaven… Why would you ever set up such a rule?

Yet we've seen so many artists who say, "I only do…" this incredibly narrow thing. If they can be creative in that space, more power to them. Even if you have a primary focus, don't let it become a shackle. Matt prefers novels in a series; Melitte prefers tintype processes. Matt also writes short stories and non-fiction like this one; Melitte also uses a point-and-shoot. And we agree that those other elements support or inspire our primary art choice.

Decide for yourself just how expansive your playspace might be. It doesn't mean that you need to discover it all at once. Perhaps for now, you play in just one corner. But at some point, your artist-self will pop its head up and peek around a new corner and go, "Wow! There's cool shit over there! Let's go!"

Chapter 2
Project Defined

Before moving on, let's talk about what a project might be. There are many different ways to do this. This is really one of those places where we need to build a common set of terms, but we'll keep it as brief and to the point as we can.

THE PMBOK

The *Project Management Book of Knowledge, 5th edition* (lovingly known as the Pim-bock) (PMI, 2013) is perhaps one of the finest soporifics ever devised. Unless you are a dedicated project manager who thinks that the intricacies of interaction between enterprise environmental factors and organizational assets in task sequencing is a fascinating problem, do *not* attempt to read this book. (Matt not only admits to being that type of nerd, but is also a certified trainer for PMI. Sad, we know.)

The PMBOK is a codification of the language used by the largest group of professional project managers on the planet, half a million strong and growing. It makes the old Microsoft *Word* manual (back when it was a printed manual) appear riveting.

It does, however have its uses and we will visit the edges of it here. It defines a project in a very simple form:

> *A temporary endeavor undertaken*
> *to create a unique product, service,*
> *or result. -PMBOK, 5th ed., p.3*

That's it. The best project managers on the planet have boiled it down to those few words. There's a reason why.

The key word here is "temporary." It is something you work on and that you complete. You'll see as we go why this is such an important aspect of it all. Being an environmental artist is a career pursued by Christo and Jeanne-Claude. A *project* was wrapping the German Reichstag or creating *The Gates* in New York's Central Park. (http://christojeanneclaude.net/)

The PMBOK goes on to break this down into ten Knowledge Areas, five Process Groups, and forty-seven distinct processes. Let's not go there.

Instead, let's consider the following, alternate view.

4-STAGE PROJECT VIEW

Consider the diagram below. We all know that projects are: started, worked on, and finished (and yes, we'll talk about projects that never seem to be finished).

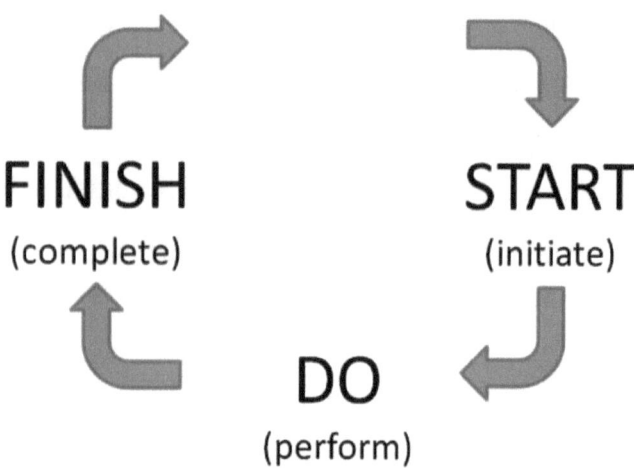

What do you suppose that fourth step might be? It isn't:
- Think up the next project –that's part of starting (or perhaps off the edge of the diagram under Project Proposal).
- It isn't marketing and selling or whatever –that's part of finishing.

One of the greatest failures of any person working on any project is acknowledging what they have achieved. Do you have an inner tape that says:
- This is so lame.
- Whatever made me think I could do this?

- This is awful! No one will want to see this.

For reasons that mystify us, both of the authors have that weakness as do most other artists we've spoken to and read about. Not only is our work *never* good enough, but we also never celebrate what we've achieved.

What if we were to turn that around? Change the language you use so that it was more like the following:

- What worked in this project that I can take forward into the next one? Both the good (what to do more of) and the bad (what to do less of).
- Wow! Did I learn a lot on that project or what!?
- Are you sure it's awful? The single worst judge of your own creation is yourself. Ask a couple of other folks that you trust. (Rarely family or friends, often not other artists. Consider finding a reader if you're a writer, a painter if you're a photographer, etc. Someone willing to be honest.)

Let's take up that last point for a moment. You are truly your own worst judge.

Why?

You had a vision of what this project could be in that "creative playspace" world. Your artist-self brought your best craft, all your skills, and all your effort to the task, but it doesn't match that initial vision. The project is deemed unworthy.

Or, perhaps, you're so proud of finally achieving something, that you can't see it for what it really is. You see the results of your work, finally embodied, created out of thin air and huge effort. It feels perfect because you see what you wanted to see in it. It's so new and shiny and pretty that you can't even see it clearly.

Enough of that, find a neutral judge. We're moving on.

So, our missing fourth element of the project cycle?

Celebrate! Revel in your success of achieving something, anything. Doing that one extra step puts us ahead of so much of the population when working with our inner-artist. Acknowledge that as well. This is your chance to pat your artist-self on the head and say, "Job well done, you!"

BROTHER'S EXPERIENCE

I wrote my first novel in 1993 and 1994. I was so proud of that manuscript that I can still remember the thrill as I lovingly printed four copies and sent it to my four best friends for feedback. It was rife with whimsy and intellectual games. It danced. It soared…

One friend has never spoken to me about my writing again. One friend simply declined to give feedback. A third stated, "This is such shit! Whatever gave you the idea you could write?" The last was kind enough to say, "Perhaps you should take a class."

I took a class, eventually I took many, and have since taught classes in a wide variety of venues. I tore apart that novel and rebuilt it, every single word, several times. Though it never matched my inner vision, it eventually sold to a tiny publisher and *The Cookbook from Hell* became the number one seller of 1997 for them.

In 2013, as a much better writer, I went back to that first pure joy and wholly redrafted the book with my vastly more practiced skills. It is a little closer to my vision now. My first readers have raved over it, we'll see in time how *The Cookbook from Hell: Reheated* sells.

I've spoken with many writers who said the day they started selling was the day they decided that everything they wrote sucks. Go figure! We are our own worst judge.

SISTER'S EXPERIENCE

Since I earn a living at photography as well as do personal projects, there's always been a meld between the two. I have experienced the ability to feel good (especially about nicely shot professional work) and at the same time have the above-mentioned, "OMG No!" moments with my personal work.

Perhaps the worst example was my first group show in Manhattan at a downtown gallery. After hanging all of my photos which were nicely matted and framed I looked around and thought, "What the hell are these photographs ABOUT anyway?"

Now at openings, just as I feel myself going to the judgment place, I try to remember that most photographers are comfortable behind the camera and not in front of a crowd. The key, for me, has been to have a core of friends who help me celebrate and actually come to look at the work.

Also the work feeds on itself. One group of pictures seen clearly in a neutral space (like not crammed into my studio) is its own type of celebration. A close look at the work and some cogitating about it brings me to a new and different viewpoint which is, as an artist, a real celebration of moving forward.

YOUR EXPERIENCE

Have you received feedback on your work, or is it hiding away somewhere "safe" from the real world? Take it to a few trusted people. Ask them for honest feedback. We'll talk about how to interpret some of that feedback safely later in this book.

Chapter 2A
Four-stage Project View
& the Artist

Hold on, didn't we just finish talking about this?

Sure, and it probably sounded pretty straight-forward. But there is another level of insight that we can describe with this simple tool. As artists, we don't just move blithely through this project cycle once we understand it. We all have strengths and weaknesses in each of these areas. Let's take a peek under the covers and see how these four stages work and what they reveal about how we can work with our strengths rather than, as we so often do, walk blindly into our weaknesses.

STRENGTH AND WEAKNESS ANALYSIS

Here's our diagram again, now completed, for easy reference.

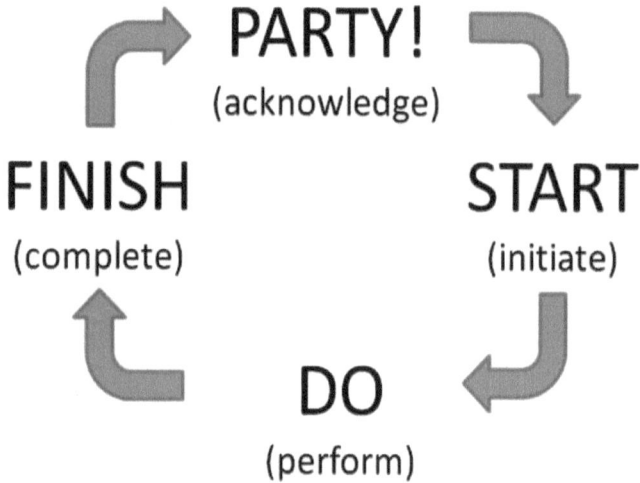

While one of the problems noted above is failure to celebrate your own achievements (never mind understand them), there are a number of other pitfalls awaiting the unwary artist, even the wary one. We each have different strengths and weaknesses when working on a project. There are signs that will help us figure out just what they are. Being too skilled at one of these four elements can be just as rife with problems as being to weak at one.

You can't start to solve the problem until you find and acknowledge it, so here are some ways to figure out where you hang yourself up in the project cycle. We'll also list the very dangerous communication that you are sending to your inner-artist.

Let's look at those various possibilities.

START / INITIATE
If you're too strong here:
- You have a HUGE file of ideas, none of which are done.
- "I have this one great idea, but I have to research it some more. I only have another three years of study before I can start."

Message to your artist-self: "I don't trust you to actually pull anything off, so I won't start on it just in case you screw up my beautiful idea with your lame execution."

If you're too weak here:

- These are the people who are always talking about how "someday soon" they'll start the project. "Just as soon as I find time."
- "I have this great idea for a book. If you could just help me write it…" Matt has had people come to him five, even ten years later with the same idea asking for help ("My idea, you write it, and we can share the profits. It's a million-dollar idea"). They could have written the book and a dozen others in that time if they had just started the project.

Message to your artist-self: "Your passion doesn't matter."

Try this:

- Take a small idea and just do it. First, starting small decreases the importance and therefore the associated mental charge. Second, it breaks the inertia.
- Matt remembers a personal growth workshop he took back in the 1980s. There was an

exercise in which the instructor is playing the warmer / cooler kid's game. You stand there with your eyes closed and as you move about, someone tells you warmer or cooler to guide you to your destination (assuming they don't tease you and keep moving the goal around—another good way to tick off your artist-self, by the way). Then, the instructor demonstrated the key point: he just stood there, and stood there, and stood there. There was no warmer / cooler information to act upon because he wasn't moving. If you don't make an effort, how will you ever know if you're getting closer to or farther from your dreams? Sure, there will be "cooler" moments—mistakes, screwups, failed projects—but at least you now know that's the wrong direction.

DOING / PERFORMING

If you're too strong here:

- This is what we call the "Redo Loop of Doom." If you find yourself on draft ten of a novel, or taking the same photograph back into the darkroom or Photoshop for the twentieth time, or…you have probably climbed on the "Redo Loop of Doom."

BROTHER'S EXPERIENCE:
I've written novels that have gone through eleven major rounds of editing. I even wrote one that went through numerous complete redrafts as in, "throw it out and start over." Despite the years, literally, that I spent on these novels, they sell in sync with my career independent of "redo" efforts. The early stuff when I was a less practiced writer, sells little to none as that was my level of craft at the time, no matter how often I revisited the manuscript. My more recent works sell better with far fewer drafts, because after twenty novels, my level of craft has matured.

SISTER'S EXPERIENCE:
Yes, I fell for this one, too. A while ago I decided to make gum dichromate prints. Then I decided to

make full color gum prints (a very involved process that includes making multiple negatives in multiple colors and registering them with pins), then I started to think that it might be a good idea to do full color gum prints on hand-made paper so that I'd really have good control of the process.

By the end of a year I'd made 2 prints.

For me the solution has been to find a process that doesn't allow me to go over that perfectionist edge. Tintype, the Polaroid of its time, is a tiny bit fussy, but there is a decisive moment where you've got about 15 or 20 seconds to make up your mind about developing the plate. It's been incredibly freeing to have to let go of control and accept a more intuitive process.

YOUR EXPERIENCE:

If it feels like you're never moving forward, perhaps you aren't. A life's work is not a single painting. (Yes, we know that Da Vinci spent years working on the *Mona Lisa*. But his creative output in other projects during that time was immense. He was an exceptionally gifted do-er.)

Message to your artist-self: "You're not good enough, I have to fix everything you do."

If you're too weak here:
- If you suffer from this weakness, you will find yourself saying such things as:
  - "I don't know what to do next"
  - "I got a good start, but I don't know what comes next"
  - "If you could tell me what to write, photograph, cast…next, then I could do it."

Message to your artist-self: "Your idea isn't worth the effort. Why should I bother with putting in the effort on what you began?"

Try this:
- This is where daily goals and other forms of motivation come in as a primary tool. We'll talk about these at length in a later chapter.
- Try breaking it down. Maybe you've bitten off too big a bite. There's an old saying: You can't edit a book, you can only edit a scene. By

breaking it down, you may see more clearly the next steps forward.
- Bottom line: Dedicate time each day or each week on creating new progress on a new project. Even if you aren't pursuing that project exclusively of all others, new progress is essential and can build into a habit of doing.

FINISHING

If you're too strong here:
- This can be the 1-book, 1-song, 1-piece of art "wonder." You've done it! You've created something so magnificent, reached so far into your skills and your soul to achieve this project that there is no way you shall ever exceed it! This is the power of finishing. Some artists are so jazzed at the finishing, that they can't restart because it's the completion where they find their energy.
- This is also where fear sets in. "I finished this beautiful thing, whatever I do next is crap."

Message to your artist-self: "I can only trust you this one time."

If you're too weak here:
- If this is you, you have a finished manuscript in the drawer that just needs a copyedit, a dozen songs sitting in a file that just aren't in the right order yet to release, or a photograph that really just needs one more round of dodging and a tweak of the color curves.

Message to your artist-self: "Sure you can work hard, but it isn't good enough to bother finishing." (We've met artists who have literally a dozen "unfinished" novels in the drawer all proofed and polished, or portfolios that are completely prepared, right down to the proper display case, but none have ever been shown to anyone anywhere at any time for any reason.)

Try this:
- If you're too strong, here, revisit the playspace idea above and go play. You may discover the

joy that got you started on the first project to begin with. In writing it's often called, "Give yourself permission to write crap." (The secret is, it typically won't be. But who's the worst judge of their own work…?)

- If you're too weak here: finish something, anything. Just declare it done and let it go. What "done" looks like will change with your field of art and the scope of that project. It could be published, released on iTunes, put up on YouTube, posted to a couple of photo-for-sale sites, etc. (A useful phrase here is: "Write and Release.")

Hint: Social Media Sharing: Think seriously about *not* putting it up for free on a social media or other sharing site. One, it could be making you money. But more importantly, by attaching a value to it—even if it doesn't sell at first—you are telling your artist-self that "I believe in the quality of your work." You'll probably be shocked at the amount of energy that was trapped in that project and is now available for a new project.

CELEBRATE / ACKNOWLEDGE / PARTY

If you're too strong here:
- You get so wrapped up in being proud of what you've done, that you never start the next project.

Message to your artist-self: "I'm more important than you are. Sure you did that great work, but I'm not going to give you another chance to do more."

If you're too weak here (this is a lot of us):
- Failure to acknowledge your successes, but rather moving directly from completion of one project and right on to the next, may seem to be the practice of a well-disciplined artist. Rather, it can lead to burn-out because you are never acknowledging your achievements.

Message to artist-self: "Why celebrate? You / we haven't done anything special."

Try this:
- Set a goal / reward. Figure out what is fun (and that you can afford).
  - When writing a book or two a year, Matt used to get a beautiful glass art float for each novel to add to his collection, a trick he learned from another writer. Now that he is a full-time writer and producing work faster, he makes a point of going out on a nice dinner date with his wife specifically to celebrate each book launch. (Their idea of a "nice dinner date" is going to a pub and playing cribbage over a burger and fries with a single glass of Tsunami Stout. It doesn't need to be dramatic, but it does need to be celebratory.)
  - Is your goal to write a short story a week for a year? Then don't promise yourself a whole pie for each one you finish unless being overweight is also a goal. Maybe you get to watch your favorite TV "guilty pleasure" sitcom only after you finish the story.

- When Melitte completes a collection, a series of images that make an artistic statement, she invites her friends over to look at the new work, to turn it into a social event. She even invites people, people whose vision she trusts, BEFORE it's ready for prime time. Getting feedback during a creative process can be a tricky business. When it works it can be a great "oh they got this one" or "yeah I can see that this one as too obscure to reach out". When she shows work there's that built-in "opening" celebration. Honestly a glass of wine and a "nicely done" from my husband is probably the best celebration.
- Maybe put a five or ten-dollar bill in a jar for each story / image and take a couple nights at a bed and breakfast at year end. Whatever motivates you and tells your artist-self that it has "done good." (Don't cheat here and tap the jar for something else because then you're telling your inner-artist, "It's okay to steal from you.")

RESTARTING

This is perhaps the most difficult step to learn as an artist. Starting a new project after finishing an old one can look like a wall towering impossibly high above you.

BROTHER'S EXPERIENCE

One of the most difficult tasks for me is restarting a new project. I remember after I completed my first novel. It was written, sold, edited, buffed, and shined. And then I sat down in front of the scariest thing there is, a blank page.

It glared at me. All white, pristine, and just waiting for me to screw it up.

I would write a paragraph and then delete it, because it was nowhere near as polished as the finished novel I had just been working on. Also, I looked at the word count. I'd just written 117 words. A novel is usually 70-100,000 words and I had 117, who was I kidding that I wanted to do that much work again. Or was capable of it, even if I wanted to.

I broke through that barrier in two ways:

- I gave myself permission to write crap. How? I went back and looked at the first words I'd written on my first draft of that novel. It was terrible. Awkward, clumsy, no decent characterization…
- I remembered how much fun I'd had doing that earlier project. I love the process of my art, the writing and exploration of it. By reconnecting to that, I remembered why I was pursuing my particular art form in the first place and how I could reconnect to it.

There is now a saying in our house that comes from a misquote out of my second novel. My wife wrote it down as "Violet is level six, start where you stand," and it became a motto of our household. "Violet is level six" is meaningless. In other words, what's past doesn't matter, be it success or failure. There is only whatever place we are standing in at this moment. Start here. (The original line was by a little girl who is singing the levels of an elevator in a spaceship, "Red Four, Green Three, V-i-o-let Six.")

SISTER'S EXPERIENCE

For some reason I've always had two projects going at the same time. The one that I'm doing and committed to completing and the one that I'm thinking about but not doing because I'm committed to completing the first one (yes, learned that one the hard way).

It is very hard to pick up where you left off once a body of work seems to have wrapped itself up. It's easier for me to work on the project that I had "waiting in the wings". On this subject I remember being very impressed by a fairy tale when I was young, something about a cobbler who heard bells that inspired him to make the most wonderful shoes in the land. Well sometimes you just don't hear the bells and you just have to soldier on. The craft needs to be kept "warm" even when you are not feeling like a creative genius.

On those days it's perfectly okay to clean the tools, mix chemicals, reorganize your photographs, or go look at someone else's work.

YOUR EXPERIENCE

Choose a project, any project, and start on it today. Now. Put this book down, and go spend even just fifteen minutes starting the next project. If you get involved and an hour goes by? We'll wait. Goethe, the eighteenth century German philosopher said:

> *Whatever you can do*
> *or dream you can do, begin it.*
> *Boldness has genius, power,*
> *and magic in it.*
> *Begin it now.*

Chapter 3
Goal Basics

"Oh no! Not another lecture on goals!"
-you at this moment

Actually, no, at least not just yet anyway. After all, we already know our goals.

I want to:
- Be on the New York Times Bestseller List.
- Become a millionaire.
- Revitalize a lost art.

- Walk a ground that no musician before has walked.
- Become known as the Modern Raku master.
- Become better at what I do.

But are those actually goals?

Oddly enough, the answer to all of these is, "No."

MEASURING IF IT IS A GOAL

Over the years, hundreds of methods of defining a goal have been suggested. There are people who have actually made a career of studying simply what is and isn't a goal. The methods below may not be the best or the most advanced. These are simply useful methods we the authors have found for measuring the validity of a goal in a way that's easy to remember.

DANIEL'S M.A.S.T. GOALS

Years ago, a speaker and friend named Daniel, who had a penchant for sailing, suggested the M.A.S.T. test for goal testing. Matt used this method for years. We can find no supporting information on the Internet and he is no longer alive to ask, so we'll assume it was his creation. He asked,

Is your goal:

- Manageable? Can it be broken down into individual tasks that have a definite beginning and end?
- Achievable? Can it actually be done by you?
- Supportable? Can you get what you need to do it, either in skills or assistance?
- Timeable? Can you put a timetable on it?

Let's take Matt's goal to be a New York Times bestseller.

- Manageable? Yes and no, but a lot of no. Yes, he can keep writing better and better books, but can he manipulate the reading and buying public into that perfect whirlwind that will get him on the list? Probably not intentionally, though there are large and very expensive marketing firms that will try.
- Achievable? Sure. Any good author can get there, eventually, with fortuitous circumstances.

- Supportable? We can even stretch this one by saying, just become a good enough writer.
- Timeable? After stretching two out of three criteria already, this is where it totally falls apart. There is no way to say, "I will be on the 2014 New York Times Bestseller List." (Not unless you're already a famous author and all your past books hit the list consistently. Even then there's some doubt.)

S.M.A.R.T.(E.R.) / S.M.A.R.T.S. GOALS

In *Management Review* (Nov, 1981) George T. Doran made what appears to be the first in-print mention of S.M.A.R.T. goals. This has grown in popularity and at present is perhaps the most commonly accepted way of testing a goal's validity. There are dozens of variations on this (http://en.wikipedia.org/wiki/SMART_criteria) that we will not explore here. Instead, we will look at our own slight variation SMARTS (as in, "Hey-yep! I's got smarts in my brains.")

- Specific
- Measurable

- Attainable
- Relevant
- Time-Bound
- Supportable (This is our own addition – stolen from Daniel's MAST.)
- The most common addition is "ER" for "SMARTER" goals and they represent Evaluate and Reevaluate to keep the goals fresh.

So, let's go back to test a different goal of Matt's. While working full-time as a corporate project manager, could he write three books per year?

- Specific: He had a definite list of titles he wanted to write.
- Measurable: Absolutely, the goal required that three new books be completed.
- Attainable: At that time it was a major stretch goal. He had written a dozen books in the last twenty years, but he'd never written so much in so short a time though he knew many people who had and did on a regular basis. It was attainable, just a challenge.

- Relevant: This is an interesting question. Is the goal relevant to what you the artist is trying to achieve? The answer was yes, as he was pursuing the dream of becoming a full-time writer (and achieved it two years later).
- Time-Bound: Yes, his plan had a 12-month deadline.
- Supportable: Yes, his skills were to the point where he could write good quality, salable stories fast enough, thus he had supported himself in preparing for this goal, *and* his family was willing to pitch in and help in any way they could including both patience and the occasional dinner tray when he was really on a roll.

It passed the test as a SMARTS goal. Did he achieve that goal? No. Why? The job totally overwhelmed him. But he did complete two books and a novella that have all since gone on to good reviews and sales. That counts as a success (one definitely worth celebrating), even though he didn't achieve his goal.

SUPPORTABILITY

Let's discuss this last point a bit more.

As writers / artists, we often feel that we are isolated. That it is somehow up to us. *And only us!* This is perhaps one of the hardest hurdles to overcome. There are many types of support and the more of it that we elicit, the more likely we are to succeed in achieving what we are endeavoring to create.

Support doesn't just show up on its own, or not very often. It must be sought and built until it is a solid platform on which we can stand. In many ways it is the third leg of the stool.

- Our Vision.
- Our Drive / Passion to achieve that vision.
- The Support by ourselves and others in achieving that vision.

In some ways it is the connecting theme of this book and the reason we decided to write it. It is about how we support our artist-self for success and how our practical-self seeks to support our artist-self.

And it can look like absolutely anything. It will be truly unique for every person, you simply need to keep an eye out for opportunities as you go. It could be:

- Taking at least one, week-long class in craft-improvement every year.
- Reading at least one book per month by professionals in your area.
- Negotiating with your family that from 6-7 a.m. is your "Do Not Disturb" writing time. Or that you get all Sunday afternoon to focus in the garage on your carving, sculpture, whatever.
- Getting your own workspace, though we know many people who create at the kitchen table or write in a coffee shop.
- Connecting with fellow professionals who share the dream to help discuss ideas, and the business if applicable.
- Friends and family who are willing to support you, not when you're having some angst fit, but rather support you in performing on-going labors in pursuit of your dream. Having a spouse who will look at you in the midst of a quiet, comfortable family evening

and say, "Go work now. We're fine." is a rare and precious thing.

Again, the list here are merely suggestions to get your thoughts moving. Your own list can take on any form. Think about what you need for success. Not what would be cool, but what you actually "need." Especially think about what you wouldn't ask for even though you do need it…then ask for it. That vastly improves your chances of getting it.

BROTHER'S EXPERIENCE
This lesson of analyzing a goal's validity really came home for me when I started taking it into the day job. "Upgrade the computer system." "Develop new job costing methodology." "Fix this department." These were often the kind of goals I was receiving from managers and they were terrible struggles.

When I spent the thinking time to upgrade my goals to MAST or SMARTS goals, the tone changed completely. "Upgrade the computer system to be Y2K compliant and remove all duplicative entry of information." "Take six weeks to create a way to bid manufacturing jobs that dynamically reflects changing material and labor costs in the estimates." "Reduce department turnover by 50% and improve productivity by 25% within 6 months." These were all Measurable, Attainable, Supportable and, especially on the Y2K project, very Timeable.

I then began looking at my creative goals, "Write a bestselling novel." "Get on the NYT list." "Make xx dollars." These didn't work and I started looking at what I could control: how much I learned, how much I wrote, and how much I marketed and published. I focused on education and practice, and I made my first novel sale a short time later after a ten-year dry patch.

SISTER'S EXPERIENCE

I think this is a case where my brother and I are assembled differently psychologically. I often see an external goal as burdensome and a "cross to bear" at best, as opposed to a motivator.

One of my greatest strengths as a photographer is that I'm always looking to connect disparate things, obscure things. I obsess about the way light bulbs work or wonder about how to reshape shadows. I especially like it when I can view something ordinary from a new "enlightened" angle.

All this can look like serious time wasting in the studio. When I have gone through self-imposed regimes of goal-oriented work it hasn't been productive, or rather what I produce hasn't been very interesting. One of my buddies had a really nice work-around that I've adopted.

It's the FIVE MINUTES A DAY plan.

No matter how busy my weekday I make sure that I spend at least five minutes either in the studio, looking at blogs, reading biographies, checking Flickr, reviewing how amazing the NASA pictures from the Hubble telescope are… You know, anything that inspires me and aligns me back with the work.

Does five minutes sometimes turn into two hours? Yes, sometimes it does, sometimes it doesn't but either way it helps me remember my commitment to my current project.

I also am very careful not to schedule my weekend days heavily at all. Once or twice a month I might go out on a non-art related mission but not more than that (well unless family is visiting of course!). An understanding spouse can make a big big difference with this. HOWEVER if your spouse is not understanding no need for divorce. You will just need to be very clear about what is "us" time and what is "me" time.

YOUR EXPERIENCE

Pull together a list of your goals. If they aren't written down, write them down as is. Then test them using MAST or SMARTS or some other method of your choice.

Don't worry if they don't pass at this point.

We just want you to get familiar with the process of thinking about a goal having definiteness, timeliness, and all of those other key elements. As you become used to using these tools, the missing elements will become easily clear. If they don't, that too is information, maybe that goal needs to be tossed and rebuilt.

Chapter 4
Finding Your Big Goal

Sometimes you already know your "big" goal. If it passes the MAST or the SMARTS test, or some other test of your choosing, great! If it is unclear, read on. Even if it is clear, this won't be that long a chapter and you might pick up some tidbits that help, so you might as well read it anyway (just saying).

YOUR BUSINESS CARD
Not the one for your day job, the one for your art. Look at what it says there.

You don't have one? Excellent! This is a great opportunity to clarify your goal at one of the highest levels (we'll talk about one step higher in the "Taking It Home and Owning It" section later in the book).

Design your business card.

For about ten dollars you can buy a pack of Avery Business Card sheets that will feed through your printer. If you use Microsoft *Word*, or most other word processors, you can simply select "Labels" probably from the Tools or Mailings menu. It will give you a design window and then you can create a whole sheet of cards. Or search the Internet for "Avery Label Templates" and their vast collection of premade templates will pop right up.

Lay out the card with your name, contact information, logo if you have one, and your job title. (You may want to leave off your home address or use a PO Box for privacy.) Designing a logo is another powerful statement to your artist-self that "this is real." However, it's a smaller impact than a business card and probably a more complex project, so worry about adding the logo later if you don't already have one.

BROTHER'S EXPERIENCE

It took me over a year to actually print out a card that said, "Writer" on it; then three more months before I could stand to hand it to anyone. I felt I was totally faking it. The fact that I had already completed and sold a novel had nothing to do with it. In a way, I became a serious writer rather than a mere hobbyist the day I printed out that card and held it in my shaking hand.

Years later, on the day that I became a full-time writer, one of the most impactful changes was taking my "Project Manager" cards out of my wallet and throwing them into recycling, but leaving my "Writer" cards in their place.

SISTER'S EXPERIENCE

My first cards stunk. Seriously, the photo reproduction was off color, the font was…well, like the font on my day job card. If you don't have good aesthetic sense look at all the business cards you can and find one that looks good to you and says "creative" or "elegant sensibility" or whatever it is that is core to your work.

Don't underestimate the importance of the look of your creative card.

Why do you have a card? You have a card to drive people to your website so don't be a Luddite, go out and mint yourself a QR code (it's free) and slap it on your card. Even more important than the card is your website. Especially if you are a visual artist, the first thing anyone will do is check you out on Google. Here's Melitte's rules about websites:

- Don't want to turn into a coding geek? If you have those skills fine, if you don't and would rather do your artwork, then pay $100 a year a get a web hosting solution. I got on this boat when I was showing a fairly well known French Scholar my site, yes he was looking at it on a PC (why I don't know) in Internet Explorer. Did it look horrible? Yes. Did he offer to become a partner in my project of the time? No. There's a number of companies that will give you choices of templates or "skins" for your site, will make sure that the site renders correctly in all of the versions of browsers and make it easy enough for you to handle simple updates yourself.

- Don't make it so perfect that it never gets out there.
- Make sure that it takes you less than 5 minutes to add a new group of great pictures.
- I beg you don't go funky with the fonts and colors. Most folks will click off a website within 7 seconds if they don't like the look. If you can use the web services templates, they hire professional geeks—if you don't like the look of the templates proceed with caution. If you've got the resources, a web designer may be a big help but remember that going that route generally makes it harder for you to do an emergency update because you just made something brilliant.

YOUR EXPERIENCE

Why is the creative-side business card so powerful? Because your practical-self has just informed your artist-self in a very graphic and real way that this is what you two are going to do together and that you both are officially good enough to move forward.

Chapter 4a
Exploring for Your Big Goal

BRAINSTORMING

There are hundreds of brainstorming techniques. We don't intend to address them here, simply to suggest avenues of research. Michael Michalko's book *Thinkertoys* has a good reputation, though neither of us has ever used it. Brainstorming can be an individual process or it can be applied in a group. Matt has used Mind-Mapping (http://en.wikipedia.org/wiki/Mind_map) in every environment from planning a novel to million-dollar corporate infrastructure project proposals. The technique also has been refined into some very specific forms as well over the years, for example as a Value Stream Map for planning Lean Process improvements. It is a very flexible tool.

BROTHER'S EXPERIENCE
A 3' x 5' whiteboard mind map of my thriller *Swap Out!* Note the central groupings in different colors: *He, She, Think Tank, Silos 2*. These were all major elements and all of the spokes off each center are ideas that connect to those central elements. Lines also connect how different elements relate to each other. Is this how the final novel came out? No, it evolved and grew, but that's part of my creative process.

The mind map is a place from which I can leap to find the creativity without having to fear I'm forgetting the interesting bits of connectivity that I discovered during the brainstorming process.

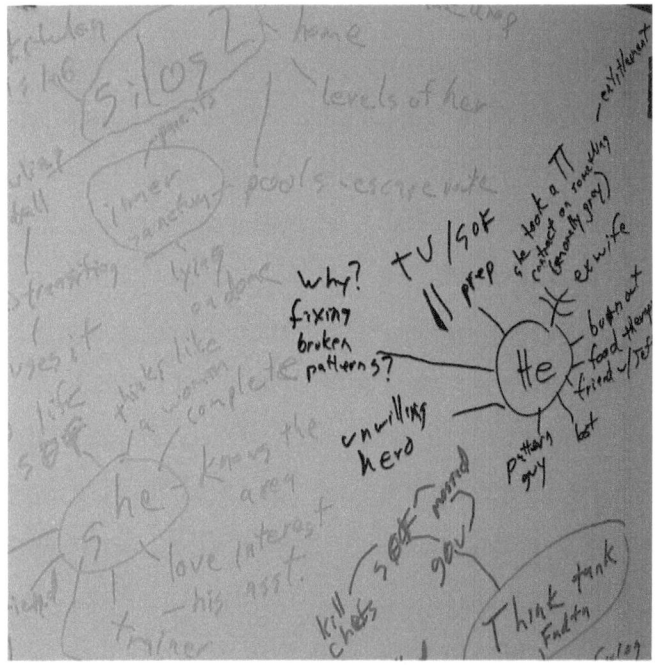

SISTER'S EXPERIENCE

My brother is so rigorous! Of course, he writes novels and I tell visual stories. What works for me is a notebook and a wall. I tack up snap shots, magazine photos, small inspiring things that I've found that are generally "like" the project I'm mulling over.

Once I get the project solidified (for example, "well everything I've tacked up has a cool shadow and that's why I'm drawn to them) I move on to the notebook. Photography is one of those crafts that needs a lot of tracking. I keep formularies, test shots, drawings of lighting arrangement, snaps of what the set up looks like. I also keep exposure times, surface treatments, anything technical that I'm likely to THINK I'm going to remember but that, actually in the critical moment a month later I'll forget.

I believe my process is different from Matt's because for me improvisation and flexibility are huge. Too much structure and it feels like a constraint, which for me generally leads to unproductive time. That said, not enough structure or goals and I can churn away in the studio without much result.

YOUR EXPERIENCE
Fool around with different techniques: Post-its, paint, free-writing, mind-mapping, whatever. The idea is to find a tool that gives you the freedom to put down good ideas as well as stupid ones. Place your "field of creativity" in the center. Find yourself torn in a half dozen directions? Put down each one and start brainstorming about how those relate or don't. You may find that what you've been pursuing has only

one or two connectors to the rest of your dreams, that's often a warning sign. Or you might find that you have half-a-dozen skills that all tie together into a very satisfying whole in a way you never imagined.

Chapter 4b
Achieving Your Goal

A KEY TO GOAL SUCCESS

In any field of study, there is something called "primary sources." This is the source of actual research upon which others build. If you're researching a moment in history, you can read the textbook version (often the least accurate), the analysis written by a modern pundit (rarely better), or delve back into the newspaper articles of the time, especially those of eyewitness accounts.

In the field of goals, there is one person who is cited by all of the modern masters. Even if they don't cite him, you can trace the source material easily once you're familiar with it. We're not saying that new work hasn't been done since on the subject, but just that the field of "success" has someone who actually did the initial research and we feel its the very best place to start.

If you investigate the roots of the excellent work done by: Covey, Robbins, Gitomer, Maxwell, Nightingale, and so many others, they all trace back to Napoleon Hill's seminal work: *Think and Grow Rich*. There is a reason that this is the number one bestselling non-fiction book in history! (…if you discount religious texts such as the Bible and the Koran, as well as the Chinese Dictionary. But still!)

Napoleon Hill spent over twenty years interviewing and studying the most successful men (and a very few women of the early 1900s): Carnegie, Ford, Graham Bell, Edison, Roosevelt(s), and over 500 others. His work has been signed off on by those people and others. Mahatma Gandhi endorsed the book giving it huge popularity throughout India.

Matt's favorite version of Napoleon Hill's various work is the audio set, *Your Right to Be Rich,* because it is a series of live lectures Hill personally gave late in his life on the key seventeen elements of success that his research identified. Primary research direct from the horse's mouth.

Another exceptional resource is Earl Nightingale's *The Strangest Secret,* forty minutes of the best audio you'll find anywhere. His information has been reused many times over the years in other works with a similar title, but this is where it came from.

Though we highly recommend it for your own benefit, this is not going to be an investigation of his research or the seventeen principles. We want to simply look at the first three elements and how they apply to working with yourself and your artist:

- A clear and definite goal.
- A burning / obsessional desire to achieve that goal.
- Applied faith. Action backed with the absolute belief that your goal is achievable.

Gee, is this sounding familiar?

He also discusses such useful techniques as forming a Mastermind group as briefly suggested above under "Supportability" in Chapter 2 and later in this book.

BROTHER'S EXPERIENCE

There is a common saying among writers:

> *"If you can quit, do! It will save you a lot of pain later."*

Beginning writers never believe this. Writing, or any other obsessional pursuit of art, can be very difficult personally and financially. It can take years of dedication and end in little more than self satisfaction, if even that. I have heard and given this advice a number of times over the years, but it wasn't until I was studying Napoleon Hill that I understood it.

It is an essential element of success that *you can't quit*. One of the three essential elements is that you need to be obsessed with your goal. So, if you can walk away from your art… Do it now! If you're still reading this book, I'll wager that you can't.

SISTER'S EXPERIENCE

Many of us start with the idea that we "want to be a [whatever]" in a very intuitive and non-logical way. I think this is fundamentally a good thing but you need to eventually be clear on WHY you want to be a [whatever].

If you want to be a photographer because it gives you great joy and helps you communicate in a fundamental way "what life is," then good for you! If however you chose "being an artist" because you were raised by a mean businessman who never had time for you and you never want to become that, then you might reconsider.

There's a family story about my Aunt Flo and her husband. Flo's husband worked in the family business, it was lucrative but he hated it. He was miserable all the time, he really loathed his job. Flo, who was always "out there" as a person, told him to save enough money to quit working for a year, find what he loved to do, OR she'd divorce him. It turns out he loved banking! Everyone was happy.

If you find that you're in the group of people who must be in the creative fields or like me must be a "maker," then know that you will have to be equally creative about how you approach financing your life.

Sadly we can't all love banking.

YOUR EXPERIENCE

If you don't have a truly obsessional desire to do something, it's probably not the right goal. Think about that. Go buy Hill's books or recordings, you'll be doing yourself a favor, both in your art and in your life.

Chapter 5
What About
All Those Other Goals

The problem that our practical-self has is:
There are a thousand other tasks, goals, and have-to's that seem insistent upon wrapping themselves around our ankles.

So, let's leave the artist-self aside for a moment and look at how to identify and work with those other goals.

TIERED BRAINSTORMING

No matter what brainstorming method you use, mind-mapping, Post-its, or a dart board, this is a method that works with any of them.

Step 1: Identify your "big" areas for personal success

Step 2: Identify at least some of the pieces that would support each of those big areas

Step 3: Choose three to focus on for now

A BIT MORE DETAIL? GLAD TO!

Step 1:

When we ask people, "What are your personal goals?" we get a broad spectrum of answers including: lose weight, make more money, find a relationship, exercise more, eat better…and the list goes on.

Great! So, make a list!

To aid in your list making, here are a few suggestions for categories, but don't feel limited by these. Try to use only 8-10 categories and fit your goals under the best heading. More than ten and the focus blurs. Less than eight, you probably aren't being thorough enough. Here's a few ideas:

- Health Physical
- Health Mental
- Finances
- Relationship
- Family
- Living arrangements
- Your Writing / Art (don't forget about that one)
- Sex
- Clothing
- Education
- Career / Job
- Self Esteem
- Security
- (Sure there are overlaps, but these are good places to start.)
- Fun, or as a friend spells it, "PHUNN!!" (she insists that the two exclamation points aren't just for emphasis but are actually part of the proper spelling of the word).

Different items will mean different things to different people. This is yet another reason that it must be you-the-practical-self working with you-the-artist-self. Just as an example: Does "Family" mean your kids, your parents, your spouse, or does it mean getting a family, or out of one?

Step 2:

Prioritize. Circle the top three most important tasks in each category. This separates out some of the chaff. Sure, owning a sports car is a fun goal, but paying off the mortgage, the kid's college loan, or your next family-togehter vacation are probably better priorities for financial goals at the moment. Or maybe not. Again, everyone is unique.

Step 3:

Come up with at least three things that would feed positively into each of these. Sure, there can be overlap, all the better! Then you get two birds with one stone. For example, Matt's mental health is vastly improved if he gets out and walks a half hour or more a day, rain or shine. That feeds mental health, fitness, weight, and relationship. (His wife often joins him and they just chat as they walk together each day—often brainstorming the next book, because she has the patience of a saint.)

Some of these categories may have a dozen or more ideas beneath them, but try to get at least three. Show you why in a moment.

SCALING

This method can be scaled easily. It can just as simply apply to life-level goals as it can to individual-project goals or even daily ones.

For example, a project might be:

> *Write and publish a novel*
> *in the next six months.*

This might then break down to:
- Brainstorming
- Research
- Writing
- Publishing

Then identify the three primary tasks under each of those:

- Brainstorming
  - Him
  - Her
  - Plot
- Research
  - Setting
  - A conflict
  - Their occupations
- Writing
  - Start writing by month 2
  - Stop researching by month 3
  - Schedule sufficient writing time for you to complete by month 5
- Publishing
  - Decide scope of publication (Amazon only or Amazon, Kobo, iTunes, Audio, or perhpas mail a query or proposal to a dozen traditional editors…)
  - Study to acquire skills or find a company to outsource to
  - Schedule sufficient publishing time to complete in month 6

DAILY PROCESS

Below are a few more tools to try. Approach these with caution. Listen to your own reaction, it will actually be your inner artist-self's reaction, as you try these out. Be willing to scoff, reject, adopt, and then later unadopt tools. You're just trying them on for size and then listening to see how your artist-self reacts. It may react quite violently to some of these. What do we mean by violent? It may simply refuse to produce any work or it may feed your guilt or your fears. Toss out that tool, try another that instead breeds excitement and hope and the thoughts of possibilities.

These are ones that have worked for us. There are many methods out there and we'll discuss others as we go.

INDEX CARDS

In his excellent recording *Goals,* Zig Ziglar suggests the idea of setting three daily tasks. Each night, scan your weekly goals list, then take an index card and write three goals on it for the next day. Work on those three goals. Whether you achieve one, two, or all three isn't the point… Okay, it's not the only point. The real key is focusing your attention on certain achievements. Simply by selecting three specific goals each day, your completion rate will increase.

Hint: Studies show that you are twice as likely to achieve a goal if it is written down.

A phunn!! tip? Keep the cards and let them stack up. It won't be long before you get to point at them and say to your artist-self, "Wow! We did all that."

LOG SHEETS

Create a daily log sheet. The example below has a place to record your three weekly goals and your daily goals. It enables you to see what tasks you are performing to meet your weekly goals. You get to Thursday and Goal #2 has nothing marked off? Time to focus on that goal a bit…or move it to the next week.

Weekly	Sunday	Monday

Or, if there are tasks that you are working on long-term, it might look like the one below. There is room here to track your primary tasks, as well as various other monthly goals. It also allows you to see at a glance how you are doing on goals such as: "I promised myself I would get in the studio at least three times this week." or "I promised myself to exercise four hours this week and I've only done three."

	S	M	T	W	T	F	S	S	M	T	W	T	F
JANUARY 2014			1	2	3	4	5	6	7	8	9	10
Exercise													
Meditate													
Write													

Log sheets can also be "art specific." These are all easy to turn into log sheets:
- I'm going to write at least thirty minutes a day.
- I'm going to take fifty new photos a day for a month just to learn my new camera.
- I'm going to paint at least three hours this week.

Here's Matt's writing log showing work on writing and audio (template available at: http://www.mlbuchman.com/innerartist password: Artist). Time is not tracked in this example, but certainly could be.

2014 Writing Log

Week of	Day	WORD COUNTS 150,000 = Yearly Goal			Consec. Days Prior yr.? 2 >411 wds/day	HOW AM I SPENDING MY TIME									FINISHED AUDIO uploaded		EXER-CISE Goal: 0.50 hours
		Words	Week Total	Month Total		WRITING Hours	Week Total	CLASS / RESEARCH Hours	Week Total	ADMIN / MARKETING Hours	Week Total	AUDIO Hours	Week Total	ALL HOURS Week Total	Hours	Month Total	
1/6/14	Mon	400			0	1.0											0.50
1/7/14	Tue	250			0	0.5				1.0							0.25
1/8/14	Wed	800			1	2.0		3.0		2.0		2.0					
1/9/14	Thu	500			2	1.0		1.0		3.0		1.8					0.10
1/10/14	Fri	200			0	1.0		2.0		1.0		1.5					0.75
1/11/14	Sat	300			0	1.0				2.0		1.5					0.75
1/12/14	Sun	250	2700		0	1.0	7.5		6.0	1.0	10.0		6.8	30.3			

TROPHIES AND QUARTERS

Make up your own system based on what motivates your artist-self.

Matt's mentor, who is quite prolific, made himself a glass globe every time he finished a book. He went to the local glass artist and learned how to do it himself. This worked for several years, until he decided that if he had any more, he'd start getting angry about dusting them. They are still a beautiful display of his success from that period.

Or write down goals on Post-its. Stick them all on a handy section of wall. As you finish them, pull them down. How fast can you empty the wall?

Or set a coin jar and some rolls of quarters by your wall of Post-its. Toss a quarter in the jar every time you take down a Post-it. When the jar is full and you can't shove another quarter through the slot, cash it in. Use a one quart mason jar with a slot in the lid (hammer and a heavy screwdriver can punch a great slot), and by the time it's full you'll have your new smartphone or a good start on a tablet.

Get creative! You're an artist, that's what you do. Find something Phunn! that motivates you.

HATE DAILY GOALS?

Are you one of these people? There are many of you out there who don't work well to daily goals. Or your day jobs don't allow work on your art except on weekends and squeezed in around family. So, tinker away until you find a method that works for you.

For example:

We interviewed several "burst" writers. They create in bursts of energy, then must stop and recharge for a time. The problem was, they weren't getting much done. Why? When we delved into it, their bursts were too far apart. So, we helped one writer begin negotiating with their artist-self.

Rather than browbeating it with charts and diagrams and daily task sheets, we had a conversation something like this:

"I create in bursts. About once every six weeks."

"Would it decrease your freedom if those bursts were more frequent?"

"As long as they aren't scheduled."

"How about this? Plan three bursts in a month. For the first two weeks, don't even think about it, just have your practical-self schedule a check-in on your calendar. When you get to the 14th, just ask yourself, 'How many bursts have I done so far this month?' If the answer is none, then you the practical-self have earned the right to give you the artist-self a sharp nudge, because the two of you made a deal to do three a month. 'You'd better get a move on, artist-self.'"

Another burst writer renegotiated their day job to four, ten-hour days. The artist-self saw the glorious expanse of a three-day long playspace and productivity sky-rocketed.

BROTHER'S EXPERIENCE

I've found that different tools help me at different times. This is where I really learned to start listening to that quiet inner artist-self. I will use a tool for as long as it works, then, when it doesn't, I'll drop it and phase in another one. I'll loop back to three index cards a day for a while, or resurrect an old checklist system. There have been whole years where I haven't used my whiteboard and then I plunge back to it like a diver gasping for fresh air. I find this to be a very effective method to keep the tools fresh.

SISTER'S EXPERIENCE

Again, I am a more organic person than my little brother. For me, entering the darkroom, heading out the door with the camera, planning to spend the day with my art, is simply a natural part of my weekly schedule.

My measure for whether or not I've been away from my art too long? I get grouchy. Eventually, my husband notices this and banishes me to the darkroom and then I start to remember that this is where I go naturally.

That said I think that adopting some of Matthew's methodology would help me be more productive—too much of it would probably piss off that "artist-self" we talked about in the beginning. I have found that focusing on a goal like "create a body of work of a dozen large prints by the end of the year" REALLY helps clarify my critical path.

For example, as much fun as testing papers is, if I have the "12 print" idea, then I'm not going to get lost in testing every art paper known to man. (You photographers out there know exactly what I mean, there are times when the process becomes more like a pseudo-scientific study and less like making something.)

Generally I make tiered goals so, for example, the current series that I'm working on I've got these goals:

- Get the work out of the box three times this year (preferably a show, but a studio visit also counts).
- Create a dozen prints (no, change that to a dozen HANDSOME prints that I can be proud of) from my current series by the end of the year.
- AFTER creating the body of work, early next year, do two different things to promote the work and expose it to people who have not seen it. Perhaps a mailer, a lecture, a portfolio review, something like that.

YOUR EXPERIENCE

Try different techniques. For three weeks, a fairly standard test period for forming a new habit, try using a checklist. For the next three, try using the index cards. Then a whiteboard, then…

SECTION II
TAKING IT UP A NOTCH

Chapter 6
Time Management
Part I

One of the most common problems we see in beginning artists and writers is how they work with time. There's a great old science fiction movie, *When Worlds Collide*. There's a prominent sign that says, "Waste anything except TIME. Time is our shortest material." And it truly is for the creative artist. Learning craft, building skills, exploring new avenues-markets-etc., consumes immense amounts of time. Where do you salvage it from? So many of us take it from exactly the wrong place, from the time we spend on our art. Well, what other options are there?

THE FIRST STEP –WHERE DO YOU SPEND YOUR TIME

Plan on having a completely normal week. Do nothing different than you normally would *except* write down *everything* you did and how long you did it. And we mean everything. Sleeping, cooking, doing dishes, driving kids around, watching TV, social media, e-mails, checking out the latest movie trailer (which on IMDB will lead to a dozen others, at 2-3 minutes each suddenly 20 minutes is gone)... Oh yeah, and record any time you spend on your art.

At the end of the week, total it up. Wild, huh?

Did you find yourself cheating? Not drifting onto Facebook for that half-hour you normally would each night, because if you did, you'd have to write it down? Or not checking out each of the dozen YouTube videos that your friends linked to you with a "Must Watch" note? That too is information.

And don't forget commuting and the day job! Log your commuting time and day job as well.

Hint: Recording your schedule in writing is also a useful tool. Anytime you find yourself not having enough time for your art, track your time for a week or a month. It will change your habits, even having to report it to yourself. That's why a common weight-loss plan is to write down exactly what you eat. Just having to write it down makes us automatically restrict wasteful eating as much as it does wasteful time management.

THE FIRST STEP SUMMARY – BREAK IT DOWN AND ADD IT UP

Look back at your major goal categories from the previous chapter. Allocate the time you're spending under the different categories. Sometimes this is hard to do, but try it, you may find it is an educational exercise.

THE TRADE-OFFS

Now that you actually know what you do, you can start to analyze what are you willing to change. This is easiest to show with real examples of what others have done. So, here's a tiny list of the many, many trade-off negotiations we have seen artists make with themselves. Again, this is a great place to let your creative self loose for a little brainstorming.

Special note: We aren't recommending any of these one way or the other. Again, try them on for yourself. For example, if you get an emotional recharge from social media, great. Knowing that will change the trade-off you make compared to someone who is drained and exhausted by social media. Always seek that which recharges you.

- We know people who have moved to smaller more expensive places because their commute went from forty-five minutes each way to five. That's an extra hour-twenty every day, times five days a week, that's six hours plus every week. That's about a 6% increase in the number of available waking hours, it is probably a significant portion of your "free" hours.
- Can't avoid the long commute? How about four, ten-hour days or a day telecommuting? You get back the full hour-and-a-half that way.

- Commuting one hour each way because he wanted to be near his kids, a friend who only got to see them once a week realized he could save eight hours per week if he lived near his job and commuted to see his kids rather than the other way around.
- Do you have a 50-60 hour per week job? How different would your life be if you found a 40-45 hour per week position?
- Watch one less TV show per night: 30 minutes x 7 days = 3.5 hours. (Is that more than you spent on your art during your "measured" week?)
- Twice per week, don't make a sit-down dinner. Just by agreeing to each "fend for themselves" twice per week, some friends freed up over an hour a week.
- Combine exercise with favorite television show using a treadmill.
- Combine exercise with favorite book using treadmill.
- Combine exercise with favorite book using audiobooks.

- Convert normal sit-down tasks to exercise at a standing or walking desk. We know someone who made her e-mail computer a stand-up machine, so that she'd be aware of just exactly how much time she spent doing e-mail rather than her art.
- If you pay a housecleaner, how much time do you gain for how much cost?
- How clean do you need your house to be?
- And here's one that's so vast and so variable, that we won't even try to address it beyond this one spot. What about cutting expenses so that you need to work less or can take a lower paying / lower stress / closer job? What would that do for your art?
  - Matt and his wife dumped their second car and saved $5,000 / year. He commuted by bicycle and combined commute and exercise for the cost of some really good quality rain gear.
  - What about dumping the house with the killer mortgage and renting or buying a cheaper / more convenient place?

- Look for cheaper dates such as concerts, parks, plays in the park. Discovering a great hole-in-the-wall Mexican place versus going back to that upscale, upcost Bistro.
- Added up the cost (or the calories) of your Chocolate Frappuccino habit lately?
- Talk to an insurance broker about your medical, car, and business insurance.

BROTHER'S EXPERIENCE

I wrote a blog religiously, twice a week for two years. My average blog was 800 words long. I wrote 210 blogs. That's 168,000 words. Two long novels or four shorter novels. Which would have paid better? Those 210 blogs or the extra novels? Once I did the math, I dropped my blog. The joke? My website now has many times more followers, and the only thing I ever "blog" there is the next book release. Go figure!

SISTER'S EXPERIENCE

Living in New York City is a real temptation. There are so many shows, concerts, lectures, all manner of cool things to do, eat, and buy. When I first moved here I probably went to two or three openings a week. I have, in some ways, chosen to be a more boring person now. I rarely go out more than once a week after work.

I do go out to lectures and shows but unless I'm going to the opening because the artist is a friend, I usually skip the opening. I mean who can see the work at an opening anyway?

This is totally counter-intuitive as many artists tell me that openings are where they work the crowd, network etc. I expect that for some people that is true but generally, for most of us, it is time that I could spend in the studio instead of drinking bad wine and feeling awkward. I guess I have a "productive evaluating meter" in my head which does a quick calculation: does doing X = a better deal than having an hour or two in the studio.

The reason this is such a big issue for me is that TIME is my least available resource. Between working and teaching (both of which I love but are still not my art) I have to be very aware of how I'm spending that resource.

YOUR EXPERIENCE
Don't try to change everything at once. We as human beings don't like change. If you want to see more about this, Google "Satir Curve" named for the brilliant therapist Virginia Satir. So, make one change from your list above. Work with it for three weeks (amount of time required to create a new habit). Then make another. Start small. The effect builds better with repeated application than wholesale houseclearing.

Chapter 7
Working with Your Inner Artist Part II

Three brief topics that we want to look at next, all related to how you spend your time:
- Identifying your work method.
- Communicating with a pinch.
- The law of diminishing returns.

IDENTIFYING YOUR WORK METHOD

We've touched on this before, but wanted to visit it one more time because it is so important.

Everyone has their own work method.

To name a few there are:

- *Steady flow artist:* Consistent day-in / day-out artists who just keep creating in a smooth, steady flow. (We have a friend who calls this the "dripping faucet," even though it gets him smacked by his steady-flow wife every time.)
- *Sprint artist.* Typically deadline-driven adrenaline junkies, they do everything except their art until, in a flash and burst and flurry of excitement, they "climb Everest" at a dead run, and then grind right back to a halt. ("Lazy, goof-off, good-for nothings" to us steady-flow artists.)
- *Burst artist.* We've mentioned them before. They are different from the sprint artist in that they are typically internally driven rather than externally "deadline" driven. They write consistently, but need breaks between to get recharged before leaping back in.

- *Deadline driven.* This person isn't necessarily a sprint writer; they have more in common with the Steady Flow folks. But they are motivated by having a deadline out in front of them.
- *Challenge driven.* Needs an escalating goal, or decreasing reward system to motivate them. A deadline may make them choke horribly, but if they select the right challenge, like the glass globes noted in an earlier chapter, they may be strongly motivated to progress forward with their art. A decreasing reward is: "I get this if I finish by then, I get a bit less if by then, and I don't get squat if it takes over this amount of time."
- *Group driven.* Some artists need their challenge to come from other artists. Novel-in-a-month challenges, weekly portfolio reviews, etc. are what motivate these artists.

There are probably many more, but this gives you an idea of what we're talking about. Now, imagine that your business-side practical-self is giving a short-fuse, crisis-level deadline to a Steady Flow, worker-bee artist. Their brains will shut down and they'll become totally blocked. You may find a way to power through it, but the inner-artist will hate every second of it and it takes all of the joy out of the process.

Why? The practical-self has just totally mismanaged their inner artist-self and the artist-self is in full rebellion. Give the same crisis to a "sprint" artist and you're in golden.

Try different methods of motivating your artist-self and watch how they react. The motivating tools may change over time, but we theorize that the essential mental structure won't change. Once a "Burst" artist, always a "Burst" artist. Your practical-self's challenge is how to discover and best manage that work method for on-going, long-term success.

COMMUNICATING WITH A PINCH

As we've mentioned, sometimes the artist-self is very vocal about how it communicates: shutting down productivity, or shouting "Yippee!" and giving you a dose of super-charged enthusiasm to send you skipping down the garden path. (Haven't gone skipping down the garden path since you were six? You should try it again. You did it back then because it was phunn!!)

But what happens when the communication isn't that clear? What happens when you do a Deadline challenge and then a Group challenge and nothing seems particularly different?

That's when we find a need to "Communicate with a Pinch." At times, the artist-self's voice is very small. It will only provide a faint feeling of "don't do that." If you aren't listening closely, you may forge on ahead because it is what you have always done. Sometimes that communication will feel like little more than a "pinch" on your conscious thought.

Matt first became aware of this while traveling solo around the world by bicycle (he calls it his "mid-life crisis on wheels"). He'd feel a small pinch and choose not to do something despite plans, and had an interesting and challenging, but also enjoyable eighteen months on the road. Then he briefly traveled with someone who had no calibration to his inner voice at all. Though they had traveled much the same ground, the other person had been robbed three times, been in a knife fight, and had numerous other problems.

Listen for that "pinch," for that little voice from within. It may be the only signal your artist-self knows how to send at first. The more you listen to it, the clearer it becomes.

LAW OF DIMINISHING RETURNS

The Law of Diminishing Returns states that the more effort / time spent on a single aspect of production will eventually decrease the overall production.

Uh huh.

Okay, try this. Which will get more success?

- Constantly revising one book until it's the best it can be

    or

- Writing not just the next book, but the next several.

Which way will you learn more?

- Constantly tweaking and tuning one image

    or

- Shooting and polishing an entire portfolio.

Let's look at what we mean by this more closely:

BROTHER'S EXPERIENCE

A book needs editing and polishing and redrafting to be a success. I won't say that it doesn't. But it can be taken to a pointless, even ridiculous extreme. How do I know? I did it.

I spent seven years writing my *magnum opus*. It took over a year to research (the full bibliography includes a hundred different books, articles, interviews, websites, etc.). It went through nine complete drafts and over a million words written and discarded, probably closer to one-point-five million.

Did I learn a lot? Absolutely.

Did my technique improve? Definitely.

Is it a better story for all that work? Maybe some. It's still the same story.

Did I learn as much and advance my career as much as if I'd written the ten to twelve books I might have during that same time? (At 80,000 words / book, a million words thrown away, the math is easy.) Ah… Hmmm… Aw, crap! No way.

That book acquired over seventy rejections before it was eventually self-published. The "Nara" series sells nicely, but nothing to brag about.

The very next book I wrote far outsells the tales of "Nara." Why? My skill level rose with more practice, but was no longer hampered by my prior words and concepts. My art had moved on a ways without me.

A friend with over a hundred novels under his belt said, "Yeah, we all have a novel like that."

Small comfort for those lost books.

SISTER'S EXPERIENCE

Oh, tweaking, that fussiness that gets in the way! Yeah I know that one all too well. Many photographers, myself included, are tweakers. "What would it look like if the contrast was higher? Maybe a matte paper?" In fact, since I make my own chemistry—it's a kind of tintype have-to, they don't really sell the stuff in photographic stores anymore—I can get lost and instead of being a photographer I could, if I allowed myself, be the crazy alchemist who tests every variable known to man. How do I know this? Because I too have done it.

I negotiate this kind of technical pseudo-science carefully because although I know that it's a weakness that I have, it is also a strength. I do tend to get interested in technically difficult processes and I tend to master them.

I am known for having exceptionally clean plates, I am a careful varnisher, I'm fussy about color balance. For me as an artist the pristine end result, the lushness of the object created, is part of what I know draws people to look at my work. What I mean is that when creating a physical object, the "container" (that is the tintype or photo-gravure or gum print) matters as much as the "essence" (the thing that's being photographed, the scene).

Although I'd like to excise that fussiness, if I did my work would suffer. So what I try and do is see if the fussiness is moving me toward my goal. Is testing final waxes going to improve the durability and beauty of the print I'm making for the twelve-print series? If yes, then I continue but if the answer is "no but it's fun and interesting" then I force myself to stop. I've learned that the goal (the twelve great prints) is what I have to be aiming for.

YOUR EXPERIENCE

Look at your projects. Are you trapped in one, long past the point of diminishing returns? If so, recognize that, then just let go and move on. Easily said, hard to do, and absolutely essential.

SECTION III
MAKING IT PRACTICAL

Chapter 8
Time Management
Part II

This chapter will look at some of the mechanics behind Time Management and how time interacts with other factors.

THE FOUR FORCES
These are typically called the "Four Constraints" of Project Management, but we don't like the negative

connotation. It makes them sound like rules as to what your artist-self is and is not allowed to do. Artist-selves hate that.

The Four Forces are not to be confused with the Four Horsemen of the Apocalypse, though sometimes it feels as if they are in the middle of a project. There are four forces that interact in project planning and execution. There are actually five, but we'll be looking at the fifth separately in the next chapter.

Here they are:
- Time
- Scope
- Cost
- Quality

It is generally agreed that if you squeeze one down, one or more of the others will move in the opposite direction. If you have less time than originally planned to spend on a project, you could choose to perhaps make the project smaller, of lower quality, or spend more, perhaps by hiring assistance.

What you can't do, except under the odd circumstance we'll discuss in a moment, is cut one force and expect the others to remain unchanged. If you add an extra room to your tree house design, either the cost is going to go up or the quality is likely to come crashing down.

It is only by being aware of these interactions, that we can begin to control them sensibly. If you save costs and sacrifice quality, you won't stay in business very long. Conversely, if you spend a little more time and / or money on a project, and the quality goes up, that could significantly benefit your success.

Again, from the prior chapter, beware the law of diminishing returns. By investing huge amounts of time or money, the quality or scope may only be marginally improved. A $2.4 million Bugatti Veyron Nocturne must be an amazing car to drive. Is it really that much better than a half-million dollar Ferrari? How about a $100,000 Tesla? All three offer an exceptional driving experience far above the norm.

While their statuses may be different to people driving in that world, to the rest of us, they're all in a single generic "super-car" class that won't get us to the supermarket any better than our 15-year old Toyota. That's the Law of Diminishing Returns and that's the trade-off of the Four Forces of the Project. You can change the balance, but doing it too far will not create significantly more benefits.

THE MATH OF PRODUCTIVITY

We're only going to give one example of this. Why? Because it is the concept that is important, but it can change completely depending on your type of art.

If your goal is to make money from your art, then being more productive will create more opportunities for you to make money. This is one of the many reasons that understanding the interactions of the Four Forces is so important. If you can create more, without a significant loss of quality or increase of cost, the more you will benefit. We can't judge for you what this interaction of factors will be, but we can guarantee that with practice, it will change.

To make your first metal weld not look like crap may have taken weeks or months of class and hundreds of failures. After a decade as a metal artist, your mind and hands are so trained that you'd have more trouble making a bad-looking weld than a clean, smooth, solid one.

To get characterization on the page of your first book is a painful process of unimaginable complexity. By the time you've written a couple of million words, that's automatic and no longer an issue. If you are actively pursuing improvement in your craft, you have other, next-level challenges that await you, but that one you have good control over.

You are not decreasing the quality, unless you become too extreme. You are simply allowing yourself to be more productive. More productivity means more to show, more to present, and more to sell, all of which makes your art more discoverable.

TIME VS. QUALITY

There is a common argument, "if you're doing it quickly, it must be crap."

You need to get over this delusion. Sometimes faster is better and does NOT impact quality, cost, or scope. Or, quite possibly, impacts them positively!

No, we haven't lost our minds.

Publishing has a tradition of one book per year, because that is all the *publisher* could handle. Then along came people like Nora Roberts who produced six books a year and has done so for decades. She has written well over 200 books, spent over 800 weeks on the *New York Times* Best Seller List, almost 200 of those weeks in the #1 spot. James Patterson is another example.

So, let's take a moment and peek behind the curtain on this one.

Prolific artists are typically living deep in Napoleon Hill's three criteria:

- Doing something they love.
- That they are obsessed by and…
- Backing it up with the action of applied faith.

This means they have practiced an immense amount, until they can lay that proverbial weld clean almost every single time.

With practice has come the skill that allows faster creation.

HOWEVER, we would argue that these criteria are only a small part of it. An essential factor of faster creation often equaling higher quality is surprisingly simple once understood:

> *Creating quickly with your artist-self doesn't give your practical-self time to interfere.*

Once the artist-self has acquired the necessary skills to at least perform their chosen art, the only thing the practical-self can really do is poke into a process it doesn't understand and screw up the whole process.

- "Is that passage good enough?"
- "You know, you can use a camera better than that."
- "No, don't do that. That's not what's marketable." As if the practical-self is wise enough to know what the potential buyer thinks would be good.

If you want to take advantage of the Math of Productivity above, get your practical-self the hell out of the way. One good way to do that, is to allow your artist-self to move fast, and keep the meddling of the practical-self to a minimum, both during and as an editor / critic afterward.

This applies even for craftsmanly type tasks, like making an immaculate image. There can be huge amounts of time wasted in second-guessing and adjusting and fussing. Yes, care is required, but there are certain elements that will be better if you allow the inner-artist the freedom to whisper, "That's right! Just like that!" and then listen closely enough and trust enough to hear it when it goes by.

THE MATH OF PRODUCTIVITY II

Here's another piece to break that slow = quality myth. Care and practice do equal quality, but speed is not really related. Again, a bit of writing math that you'll have to adapt to your own art and craft.

- The average writer can type around 60 words per minute.
- Most writers report writing (vs. typing) between 750 and 1,000 words per hour.
- Doing the math, 1,000 words / 60 minutes = 17 minutes of typing per hour. (So, to

write 1,000 word per hour is 17 minutes of typing at full speed and 43 minutes of staring thoughtfully into space.)
- An 80,000 word novel can therefore be typed in 80 hours on average. Double that for editing and redrafting, and add another factor again for research if you wish. For an investment of 240 hours (that's just 6 weeks at 40 hours / week), you have produced a novel, and spent a significant portion of that time staring thoughtfully into space.

Think about your art. Do the math. Math is great for busting myths for both the practical-self and the artist-self.

Acknowledge that there is a skill you have acquired that allows you to be more productive and that has value. There's a story of a retired machinist who was called in to fix a factory, some fault that no one else could find. He spent a few hours walking through the factory then put a white-chalk "X" on a piece of equipment and said, "Replace that." He sent a bill for ten thousand dollars.

When his employer protested, he revised the bill: $1 for chalk, $9,999 for knowing where to put the "X." His bill was paid without further complaint.

Hint: Never tell a non-artist how fast you can do your art. They won't believe you and it will devalue it horribly in their eyes. We know that the secret to art isn't how fast you perform this particular piece, it is the decades of practice you put into learning your craft that allows you to move more rapidly. But there's no way to explain that to the non-artist.

COST OF INTERRUPTIONS

We've touched on this briefly before, but it bears repeating:

Interruptions are very expensive!

They have numerous costs. Some of which are easy to measure like the eleven-minute loss of productivity found in computer programmers. Some are not easy to measure, like the time lost when a flow is broken and must be reconstructed before you can continue.

The Harvard Business Review has an excellent blog on this topic (http://blogs.hbr.org/2011/12/how-to-accomplish-more-by-doin/). We particularly like the cited article in *Psychological Review* (http://www.definingsomeday.com/wp-content/uploads/2010/05/EricssonDeliberatePracticePR93.pdf) where a study at the Berlin Academy of Music revealed that a 90-minute work span was deemed the most constructive among concert violinists. We have a friend who works as an efficiency expert for a large computer software corporation. His own studies have consistently confirmed significantly improved production with 90-minute uninterrupted sessions, separated by 5-15 minute breaks.

The measurable productivity improvement during an 8-10 hour day is on the order of 30-40%!

BROTHER'S EXPERIENCE

I use a timer to work in 90-minute sessions and have seen significant improvements in both my output and comfort. I used to work in big massive sprints that would leave me a physical wreck, often for a day or two afterward. "But it's the only day I have to write all week, I can't waste a second," I'd tell myself. When I was really at the peak of a story, I could write about 5,000 words in 5 hours, or 8,000 words in 10 hours.

Once I read the violinist study, I did a little testing of my own. Here's what I found were my results.

- 60 minutes = 1,000 words
- 90 minutes = 1,750-2,000 words
- 2 hours = 1,500-1,750 words

Yep, my productivity actually went down because I "knew" I was working to a longer session. And I often write as much from 60-90 minutes as I do in the first hour because I'm both "on a roll" and "trying to get it done before that 90-minute timer goes off."

Now that I have my 90-minute habit, I recently had occasion to do a 4-hour session without any break. I produced 3,700 words, most of them in the first two hours. Lesson learned.

I had to leave this book briefly to work on another deadline. What I'm trying now that seems to be working even better is a 45-minute session, stand up and stretch (rarely even leaving my office), then

45 minutes more. Then a 5-10 minute break. My body feels better and my productivity is up another small notch.

SISTER'S EXPERIENCE

My sessions are unregulated. I find there is a natural rhythm to my work. If a timer goes off when I'm 99% of the way through a print, it's just going to make me angry. However when I analyze my best working pattern, it's when I am most productive and, frankly, happy. That, if you will, is my own timer.

I find that my art is a variable but intense process. Setting up the shot, preparing the chemicals, final focus, processing, looking at the results, making some changes, and redoing if necessary. That is the process itself, though it has more varied activities associated with it.

But the key element is the "happiness factor" (HF). When I'm balanced and interested time flies by. Unfortunately, since my time in my studio is limited, there are days when I just feel pressured to produce. When I'm outside of the HF, I tend to spend too long in the studio, and enjoy it less.

YOUR EXPERIENCE

Make the same experiment Matt did. Prove it to yourself and prepare to be amazed by the results.

Chapter 9
Risk Management

WHAT IS RISK MANAGEMENT

Project Management is a learned skill, just like any other craft.

At the simplest levels you discuss scheduling and resources. As you advance, you begin to understand and work with the Four Forces. At the higher levels, you look at full life-cycle management; rather than just project execution, you begin facilitating how planning, execution, controlling, and completion all interact. (And celebrating if you're being smart about it.)

But if you get a group of 20-year project management veterans off in a corner somewhere, you'll hear them talking almost exclusively about managing risk. What are the risks to cost or scope if we make this choice? How do you plan for the unanticipated risk, because you know from experience that it will show up? Why weren't you able to predict a risk earlier and how can we understand that in order to decrease the next project's risk?

So let's talk a little about this highest level of project management.

POSITIVE AND NEGATIVE

Brad Hermanson, one of the nation's leading environmental risk assessment specialists, pointed out two very interesting things to Matt:

- No one ever plans for the Black Swans.
- No one ever plans for positive risk.

Okay, a little explanation is required here.

Black Swans

A Black Swan is an event that "is as rare as a black swan." These are the true outliers of project management. Here are a few examples to show what we mean. Are you prepared for these?

- A writer's house burned down. He lost every word he'd written up to that moment except for a few short stories he'd finally begun selling. The only copies of multiple novels, a hundred short stories, and reams of poems were lost. This was back in the days of paper and typewriters, but carbon paper and copiers existed. He didn't even have a fire safe. To say that he makes a nightly backup onto a USB drive and puts it in his car's glove box every night is only the least of what he now does.
- A writer lost four novels when their harddrive crashed unrecoverably. They had been backing up onto their USB, but they hadn't replaced the backup right away after losing the USB the prior week.
- A writer went on vacation and the dam above her house broke. Her house literally washed

away. She lost everything, except her writings. She had both a laptop and a backup with her.
- Famous writers, both of novel and screen, are sued all of the time by people who claim that their bestseller was not their idea. And they hold aloft a tattered sheaf of paper twenty years old to prove it. If you don't have insurance (and you are innocent), you'll be defending yourself out of your own pocket. Business insurance can solve much of this risk exposure.

Designs, images, plans, writings… What have you done to protect yourself against Black Swans? Planning for a risk and how to manage it beforehand is called Risk Mitigation for those of you who want to get more into it.

Positive Risk
This is a funny one. It's the "Doh!" moment among project managers as they move toward that highest level of becoming risk managers. There are two primary aspects to positive risk:

- Planning on what to do if you succeed.
- Planning for unexpected opportunity.

We see the failure of the first one all the time. Look at the disasters created by Hollywood stars who strike success young. And look at lottery winners, some studies state that as many as 70% of those who receive windfall levels of money wind up broke, even bankrupt, meaning their final financial situation is even worse than before the windfall.

Plan for success. If you had a novel or screenplay or piece of art go blockbuster and you received a million dollars for it tomorrow, would you know what to do with the money? U.S. banks only guarantee deposits up to $250,000. Did you even know that? Do you have a spending and investment plan?

Hint: Create a written plan for success. Start building relationships with people more successful than you. Don't talk with them about craft, talk with them about business management. Ask them about financial planning, business insurance, industry knowledge. Because we can guarantee that's what top-level professionals are discussing when they get together. Read Anthony Mancuso's book from Nolo Press, *LLC or Corporation*. Make sure your will is in order, and your medical insurance. Read Kristine Kathryn Rusch's *The Freelancer's Survival Guide* and pay attention to her checklists of good practices.

The slightly more elusive, but potentially lucrative aspect, of positive risk awareness and planning, is being prepared for the unexpected opportunity. What if your career finally takes off, are your supply chains in place so that you can manage that success?

You're an indie artist and you've been selling music / art / books through your website, what happens when it takes off and you receive ten thousand orders? Did you plan sufficiently to take advantage of the opportunity, or are you going to have to shut down the website because your laptop is too slow burning CDs and mailing has become your full-time job? Or, perhaps even worse, will you be forced to spend so much time on the business of your art that you no longer have time to do your art?

Both of these types of positive risk require flexible plans and also close attentiveness to make sure that opportunity doesn't slip by unnoticed.

UNDERSTANDING COSTS OF CHOICES

Very simply, every choice has a cost. Do I take a class? The class costs money *and* time away from creating my art. Do I work on this piece next, delaying the other?

"Costs" are not just money. They can include time, stress, patience, impact on the family, and dozens of other factors. We have a friend who coined a very important phrase. Matt was designing and building a solar-electric powered home. He was adding more and more features to the design when his friend suggested:

Protect the Family Environment

It simplified the house design, saved money, and made it so that the family wouldn't need to become solar engineers to live in their own house. Family is a key cost to consider.

We can think of no way to explain this without delving into each unique art. So, we will simply leave it be other than to say, an awareness of those costs is essential in deciding which path to choose. This is where the practical-self really steps into control and says to the artist-self, let's go over here and tackle this together.

Hint: Did you notice what we did in that last sentence? Cooperative language. "Tackle this *together*." Think about the language you use with your artist-self, it can wholly change your results. If we had instead said, "You need to work on project X now no matter how cool and shiny project ZZZ looks." How different an emotional response that elicits. Be very conscious of language when communicating with your artist-self.

ADDING RISK AS THE 5TH FORCE

Risk really is the fifth force (fifth horseman of the Apocalypse?). When increasing scope, from a 20-piece show to a 25-piece show, what additional risks are you incurring? Additional shipping costs? Lower quality of the last three pieces because you really didn't have the time to make 25?

Factoring risk into those decisions is essential. But is there an easy way to do that? Risk Managers frequently use SWOT diagrams for exactly that reason.

SWOT ANALYSIS –EIGHT SQUARES TO UNDERSTANDING HOW YOU MANAGE TIME

Some people prefer graphic tools, rather than the whole mess of words we just offered here. So, let's look at a SWOT analysis—SWOT stands for: Strengths, Weaknesses, Opportunities, and Threats. A simple SWOT looks like this:

	Positive	Negative
Internal	Strength	Weakness
External	Opportunity	Threat

We can change what we're looking at just by changing the two axes (why the plural of axis can be used for chopping down trees is just another oddity of the English language). In Risk Analysis, the diagram will more typically look like this:

	Low Negative Impact	High Negative Impact
High Importance	Plan for mitigation	Fix this

But we're going to suggest something like this is how you should really use this diagram:

	High Importance	Low Importance
Awesome	Drive for this!	Shouldn't be

To make use of this diagram, take your vast list of tasks that we made back in Chapter 5 and map where they fit. If you are working on lower-row tasks when there are still upper-row tasks to do:

CUT IT OUT!

BROTHER'S EXPERIENCE
The worst case I ever saw of non-use of a SWOT-style analysis involved a Boeing engineer. He had taken a three-month sabbatical to complete and really polish his science-fiction thriller. We had a dinner at his house about halfway through his sabbatical. He had spent the last three days sanding the inside of his medicine cabinet and getting the new paint to have just the right finish.

I wish I was making this up, but I'm not. He said, "I just couldn't focus on the writing while knowing there was this bit of rust in the corner of the cabinet." To the best of my knowledge the novel, which was complete and told a good story, was never "finished" or marketed.

SISTER'S EXPERIENCE

I've seen hundreds of artists fall by the wayside over the years. Each one's reasons are different and each one is valid, to them. What I have learned is that for an outside person to point out how they are sabotaging themselves rarely helps and often elicits anger. That recognition must come from within.

We have a mutual friend who talks about coming from a family of addicts, and she consciously chose to become addicted to her art as a far healthier alternative. I think there is a lot of truth in this for many artists, but, like other types of addicts they have to admit there's a problem before seeking help solving it.

We've finally concluded that each artist must find their own path. Our hope in writing this book is to offer tools to try out if you find you're walking down that path in the wrong direction. If it's a friend you see doing that…Well, you could try slipping them a copy of this book…

YOUR EXPERIENCE

Take your to-do list from the earlier chapters and plot it on the SWOT diagram. Draw the boxes on a whiteboard and stick up your Post-its or whatever method you choose. Now, use their relative importance and impact to reconsider the priority order of what you're doing.

Hint: Tackling a high-impact task can take a lot of effort and energy, so mix them up a bit. Take on one high-impact and two low-impact tasks for your three goals that week.

Chapter 10
The Action Plan

Now it's time to put together an Action Plan. This serves many purposes:
- A goal is twice as likely to be achieved if written down and shared with a friend (http://www.dominican.edu/dominicannews/study-backs-up-strategies-for-achieving-goals). Also read Napoleon Hill's chapters on the power of the Mastermind group on this topic.
- You'll sleep better, rather than worrying that you've forgotten something crucial.

- Your artist-self will know what's coming next, so they won't get surprised or shocked.
- Your practical-self will love it.

WHY IT'S IMPORTANT, BUT IT'S NOT

Hint: It may be written, but it isn't written in stone. Plans can be revised as new information is factored in.

A written plan is not an iron-clad contract. Let's look once more at Napoleon Hill's three factors from all the way back in Chapter 4:

- A clear and definite goal.
- A burning / obsessional desire to achieve that goal.
- "Applied faith" or action backed with the absolute belief that your goal is achievable.

Notice what's not there? A plan! Why not? Because a plan can be altered without changing your ultimate goal. Try things. If they don't work, scratch them off and try something else. A clear eye on your goals will keep both of your-selfs focused on getting it done. Your job as a practical-self is to keep trying new things to help your artist-self.

A FEW ORGANIZATIONAL TIPS
- Consider contractual deadlines first. Did you make a commitment to deliver a piece, put up a show, restock something? This is a contractual obligation, do this first. Better yet, get it done ahead of schedule in case something unexpected Black-Swan's in.
- Focus on your strengths. So many classes seem to talk about bolstering your weaknesses. How about focusing on your strengths? They're what got you here in the first place! A great free reference on this is a talk led by Marcus Buckingham and Oprah Winfrey "Take Control of Your Career and Your Life" (iTunes podcast or http://www.oprah.com/money/Marcus-Buckinghams-Career-Intervention).
- Bolster your weaknesses. Yes, patch the weaknesses, but run them through a cost analysis first. As a professional writer, Matt is always looking at what he can improve. However,

there are marginal, low-return classes that would help, but they would cost valuable writing time. He often instead takes a class in a strength, but taught by someone much farther down the road than he is.
- Fast Track. This is a project management phrase. What it means is, to do tasks simultaneously that don't conflict. While we recommend working on only one creative project at a time, that doesn't mean you can't be:
    - Doing research for a future project.
    - Working on the current project.
    - Polishing and packaging the latest project.
    - Marketing the latest released project.
- "Admin is always getting in my way!" Ours too. How about scheduling an "Admin Evening" once a week to deal with the business of your art? Make it a regularly scheduled appointment. Matt has made a deal with his artist-self that Mondays belong to his practical-self. "Admin Mondays" is when he works exclusively on admin that day until he has caught up.

WIBBO

Writer Scott Carter (http://scottwilliamcarter.com/) came up with the WIBBO test. Actually, he named it the WIBBOW test, but he's flexible. What it stands for is:

Would I Be Better Off Writing?

In its WIBBO form, you may tag your own art form on the end. "Would I Be Better Off Behind the Camera?" "Would I Be Better Off Carving?" "Would I Be Better Off Composing?"

It is sort of the ultra-simplified version of all of the risk analysis questions above. It is a critical question in developing your action plan. WIBBO conveniently tests every decision in just a moment's thought.

Perhaps the best part of it is, it is one of the few controls that your artist-self has on your practical-self. The artist-self is normally left to communicate by reaction only: think project-block or "Whee!" reactions. What Scott created that is so awesome is a way that the practical-self—who always sees a thousand things to do—can ask the artist-self what the best next step is.

Only rarely does an artist-self abuse this; it's usually too shocked at being asked at all. The abuse might look like constantly producing, but never releasing. Again, back to our friend with a dozen finished novels in the drawer. The cure is simple, showing the artist-self the joy of releasing art into the world. (See earlier discussion on what you're telling the artist based on strengths and weaknesses of the 4-phase project diagram back in Chapter 2A.)

BROTHER'S EXPERIENCE

On a daily basis, it is using the WIBBOW(riting) test that gets me back in the chair and writing. Am I wading through leaves to get to the front door? Yeah, shoulda raked a couple weeks ago. Would I like to rewatch that old favorite movie? Sure. Should I go exercise? (Okay, not that last one so much.) But it is a simple tool that I use to constantly remind myself of what's important: practicing my art. It even gets me out of "terminal researchitis" when I've gone too far down that slippery slope.

SISTER'S EXPERIENCE
I still work full time as a digital archivist, a job I love and has the extra advantage of payment and benefits. When I find those precious hours to work on my art, I don't even need to ask the question, I just go to whatever is next. Planning a shoot, ordering chemicals, printing, or perhaps preparing for a show. WIBBODoing-what's-next? I already am.

YOUR EXPERIENCE
Write "WIBBO" on a half-dozen sheets of paper in big, block letters. Tape them up at strategic places in your home and playspace. Perhaps even on your lunch bag. Would you be better off sitting with a bunch of people you'd never willingly associate with outside of work, or taking that same 30 minutes to read Napoleon Hill, study a book of technique, or even do some writing or design work at your desk?

Chapter 11
Working with Your Inner Artist Part III

Some of these will feel like repeats, some of them intentionally are. We're trying to bring these important parts into daily practice.

BUILDING DISCOVERABILITY

One of the key challenges for any artist is being discovered. We aren't going to go into the many and various possible techniques for doing this.

However, it is worth mentioning that your artist-self loves the idea of being discovered. It will send your practical-self off in search of a thousand shiny rainbows because maybe that will create that great day. After all, some marketing pundit, friend-artist, third cousin, etc. swears that it is, so it must be.

The thing to convince your artist-self of is that the best way to improve discoverability is to create more channels to be discovered by. Remember that chart in the earlier chapter about increasing income by increasing production. Remember this when working with your artist-self. The real payback is in creating a critical mass.

Yes, your work must be discoverable to be found, but that is the purview of the practical-self. Your practical-self must do their job to make sure that your mutual art is available and well-announced or risk insulting the artist-self. It is your artist-self's purview to create more for your practical-self to market. Again, making it a team effort will keep both parts of you content…as content as any artist ever is.

PROPOSALS

Don't you hate having a thousand ideas and knowing you need to focus on just the one in front of you so that you can get it done. Is your artist-self always rushing off to some new project? How do you satisfy your artist-self's need to be heard versus your practical-self's need to retain the focus on the current project?

Well, if you have a traditional publisher, what you would do is write a proposal. If you were an artist, you might write a grant application. A musician might swing a mike into place and record a likely riff along with a rough verse and chorus. And so on.

Do that. Have your artist self send a proposal to your practical-self. Full-on, just as you would in the real world.

This lets the artist-self return to the current project without fear that the idea will be lost. The idea is captured, but the practical-self / manager gets to say that the time isn't now.

BROTHER'S EXPERIENCE

I allow my artist-self to have three hours to write a proposal. It includes a brief synopsis based on whatever ideas came together to make me think this would make a great story that I wanted to tell. Then, I usually have a scene or two that would make a good introduction to the characters, tone, and setting.

In three hours, I can write the synopsis and 5-8 pages, exactly what I would send to an editor. This lets my artist-self get it out of its craw and place the course of action back into the practical-self's hands.

Then, when the current project is finished, the practical-self can flip through the various proposals—perhaps considering marketing and scheduling and other things the artist-self doesn't care about—and say, "How about this one next? You liked this one."

SCHEDULING CREATIVITY

"You can't do that!"

Ah, but you can. Not only by scheduling 90-minute "creativity sessions" or "creativity days" as suggested earlier. If you can schedule it at regular times during each day, productivity typically increases. Believe it or not, most artist-selves that we've interviewed like predictability, despite how flaky we think they might be.

BROTHER'S EXPERIENCE

I began writing on July 21st, 1993. I was on a plane from Korea to Australia on a round-the-world solo bicycle trip I mentioned earlier. I started a story in my journal that became my first novel, *Cookbook from Hell* (now wholly redrafted with much better skills as *Cookbook from Hell: Reheated* that I mentioned earlier in this book). I finished the first draft in February, 1994 in India. I took a class in 1995.

It was the third week of that class when I decided that if I was going to be serious, I needed to act serious.

A dedicated night-owl, able to leap from bed, shower, dress, and be out the door with a bagel between my teeth in under four minutes—because that bought me three more "snoozes" in bed—I reset my alarm clock for two hours earlier. To this day, those first three weeks still rank as utterly miserable in my memory. I wrote for an hour-and-a-half every morning, a habit that has survived mostly intact through the last twenty years.

My artist-self latched onto those morning sessions as belonging to it and it alone. Lord knows, nothing else was going to get me up at that hour.

The day I turned back my alarm clock is the day I became a writer.

SISTER'S EXPERIENCE

I made no grand transition as my brother did from Project Management to creative writing. In college, I entered as a Geology major and departed as a Visual Arts major, eventually earning my MFA in photography. Since that time, art has been an integrated element of my lifestyle, both in job and hobby. Even my greatest aberrations, a number of years as an Office Manager, I was managing the offices of highly successful artists or art services companies.

There is no "day" that I became a photographer. Nor any moment that needs to be scheduled to maintain focus. It is what I am and what I do; my art is an integrated element of who I am day to day. I have tried / will try several of the things my brother has mentioned… But perhaps we're that different. Or perhaps when I pursue my art as a full-time livelihood. Or perhaps never. Sorry, Matt.

For now, what I am doing works for where I am now.

YOUR EXPERIENCE

Trying scheduling a consistent block of time to be creative in. Whether it is daily or every Saturday morning doesn't matter. Try it for three weeks. We think you'll be amazed at what happens during that time once your artist-self sees the pattern for regular creativity.

SECTION IV
TAKING IT HOME AND OWNING IT

Chapter 12
Core Principles:
why you do what you do

There is a TED Talk by Simon Sinek (http://www.ted.com/talks/simon_sinek_how_great_leaders_inspire_action.html) and his book (*Start with Why*) that we very highly recommend. He asks a critical question:

Why do we do what we do?

This is one of those very deceptive questions that can be extremely difficult to answer. It can take months, even years to arrive at the answer, and I'll point you to the works of Simon Sinek for assistance.

"But why do we care?" you might ask.

We write, paint, sculpt, perform, compose, weave, create (or in some cases destroy), hide, reveal, and a hundred other variations. Yes, we do all of these things, so do thousands of others, hundreds of thousands. There were over a million new titles and editions of books published worldwide in 2012.

Everybody's doing it.

As Simon Sinek teaches us, what makes you different from others, what makes you unique, is "Why" you do what you do.

"How can you be unique among the masses?"

What makes us unique is our own personal "Why." It is what makes us consistent as artists, it is that element of our artistic voices that others wish to hear. It is also the "Why" that is the *ultimate* litmus test for our artist-self.

Some examples:

- Matt's – "To champion the human spirit, the power of joy, and the wonder of love." If a story doesn't fit all three of those criteria, he doesn't write it because that is the core "Why" that motivates him and his artist-self.
- Another writer – "The Entertainer." Just that simple. But deep inside that writer it strikes a whole chord of feelings and emotions that give his stories a unique feel and flavor. He is so practiced at including his "Why" in his stories that you can pick up any of his hundreds of publications and the threads of "The Entertainer" and his interpretation of that "Why" are laid like pulsing veins of life throughout.
- Another – "To experience and share exciting people, places, and things."

"There can't be a million different ones of those!" I can hear you exclaim.

Are you sure? Besides, if another person picks up "To Champion the Human Spirit" and the author knows of several who have hijacked it with Matt's blessings, it is going to be expressed through what it means to them.

Your "Why" is the expression of your core values. Are you screwed if you don't know what it is? Not at all, because your artist-self probably already knows. If you wander away from your artist-self's "Why," what do you think happens? Yep! Slow-downs, uneasiness, a pinch, or "project block."

If you know your "Why," you can avoid this oh-so-common artist's malady.

BROTHER'S EXPERIENCE

I didn't land on "To Champion the Human Spirit" all at once. I had to ask myself questions like: What story do I want my art to tell? What is important to me? What is unique about my world view?

Once, as part of a writing workshop exercise, I came up with a brilliant and chilling villain. He totally creeped me out, by far the nastiest most awful character I've ever run into in millions of words of writing. For a decade now he has begged for his book…and he's never going to get it.

Why?

Exactly, because he doesn't fit my "Why." I don't want him in my thoughts, in my house, or in the words and images I put into my reader's minds. He is the precise antithesis to all of the reasons I write (which was, appropriately enough, the instructions of that class).

And if I were to try and write him anyway, I'd wager that I would land in the center of the next section, "Project Block."

SISTER'S EXPERIENCE
Although I don't have a verbal statement (that visual part of me can be stubbornly…umm, visual I guess). There is without a doubt something that includes wanting these things:
- Sharing a sense of renewal of self.
- Longing for belongingness.
- Raising up (in some sort of über sense).
- What I see and want to communicate that I cannot use words for.

There are also things that I will not photograph. I'm not sure what it would be called: visual ethicality?

There are very photogenic moments both with people and landscapes that are ethically charged for me. I will not mock. I will not "take" an easy target. I've always felt this is core to my work and that violating it would have dire consequences on my ability to make work.

I know that in some ways this limits me, but I also know that is who I am. There are plenty of "see how messed up this is" photographs out there. I do not want to be one of the people making them. There must be some "Why" to this behavior. (Brother's note: just look at the first three of your criteria above, sis. The "Why" is laid out right there.)

YOUR EXPERIENCE

If you wish to pursue this tool, start with Sinek. He will prompt some interesting thinking.

Chapter 13
Project Block

WRITER'S BLOCK

Everyone has heard of "Writer's Block" and, by extension, any artist may talk about how, "They are totally blocked." We would argue that there is no such thing, at least not in such a broad, all-reaching term. Oh, there might be external circumstances: family emergencies, moving, new jobs, and all the other well-known, high-stress situations. These can last days, or in the case of extended illness or landing in the caretaker role of someone incapacitated, years.

However, that isn't "Writer's Block." That is plain and simple overwhelm. When we are through those stress-causing conditions, we can once again pay attention to our art. We might even suggest that the way through such times is specifically the practice of your art. Even if only a half-hour per week, it may be a promise to your artist-self that there will be light ahead.

"Then if it isn't Writer's Block, what is it?"

PROJECT BLOCK

Is there some reason that specific project has stumped your artist-self? For that is the experience of dozens and dozens of people we have discussed this with.

There are any number of reasons for Project Block:

- Your concept is beyond your present skill level. It helps if you recognize this before jumping off the deep end and losing yourself. For example, Stephen King, while still in his teens, decided he wanted to write a multi-volume epic-fantasy saga. He specifically set aside the "Dark Tower" series concept because he knew he wasn't ready. He finally started it in his thirties and completed the series in his late-fifties. He states that while he had the skills to begin it when he did, he still had to wait and practice until he had sufficient skills to complete it.

- You don't know enough yet to do that project. Some works simply require a lot of research. And if you insist on attempting a work without placing understanding behind it, your artist-self will just sit down and stick its tongue out at you.
- The project is "boring." No, this is not an excuse to hop from one project to the next to the next. This is probably a project chosen by your practical-self that your artist-self doesn't give a damn about. Figure out where you went off track, discard that single project, and choose the next more carefully. Or, if you're already committed to that project, make a deal with your artist-self, "You finish this one, and

you can play with the next one." That tactic may work, but it may still be a struggle.
- The project doesn't meet your internal "Why" mentioned in the previous section. You may not know, but your artist-self always does and can be extremely stubborn on this point.

These are the primary ones we've identified, though we're sure there are others. Most "Writer's Block" boils down to stress overload. Most "Project Block" boils down to tangled communication with or expectations of your artist-self.

PROJECT STALL
"Project Stall" should not be confused with either of these. A project can stall from something as simple as the artist-self running out of ideas at the moment, or just being plain tired.

A few ways out of Project Stall:
- Go back and read the studies mentioned in Chapter 8, *Cost of Interruptions*. Try a session-based work schedule. One writer told us that after 55 minutes, his brain just

shuts down. He gets up, gets water, a snack, plays with the cat, almost anything, and then his artist-self is ready for another 55-minute session.
- Plan for it. Matt does two creative sessions, then goes for his daily exercise walk. Then a production or business session, then another break and only then another creative session.
- Ask your subconscious for help. This technique, discussed at length by Napoleon Hill, suggests giving your subconscious directions on creativity before a nap or sleep. By posing yourself a specific question, often the answer will present itself.
- Whiteboard the problem. Take markers and start brainstorming. Put down what you know and what you don't know. Write the sensible, the absurd, and the absolutely ludicrous.
- Try to explain the problem to a non-artist. It's amazing how often they'll ask the most naïve question that launches you right out of your stall. They'll probably look at you as if you were a certifiable nutcase when the next-step

answer comes crashing into your conscious mind because you'll start your Victory Dance, but it's worth it.

- Fake it until you make it. A growing adage among a group of writers Matt works with is: "Just write the next line." Eventually, you will write past the stall. So what if you had to throw out a chapter, a print, a verse. If you climbed out of the Project Stall, you'll be more productive climbing out of it than if you had wallowed in its depths.

BROTHER'S EXPERIENCE

I miss mowing my lawn. We used to have a half acre or so of lawn. It wasn't pretty, it was just field grass on rough ground. But when I'd get stuck, I'd go out and mow and just let my mind wander.

Frequently, the solution to my problem would come crashing in and I'd just shut down and abandon the mower right where it was. Sometimes my wife, knowing this was my "thinking chore," had to haul it back to the shed as I'd completely forgotten about it. Occasionally it took me weeks to mow the lawn, all in these little fits and starts.

SISTER'S EXPERIENCE

I've got a couple of strategies when this happens. Tidying up the studio, mixing chemicals, organizing negatives is a favored activity when I'm stuck. Going to a museum to look at work—generally non-photographic work—is also a strategy for me when I'm stuck. Sometimes just taking a picture a day for a week, and not judging whether they're good or bad helps.

I agree with Matthew though, if you are seriously stuck, especially as you're getting going on a project then you may have convinced yourself mentally that it's a good idea, without the substance of a truly felt project. This never works out well, I know from experience.

YOUR EXPERIENCE

Try different techniques. Are you a writer? Try a watercoloring break. Are you a musician? Go sew on a bedroom quilt. Give instructions to your subconscious then go ride a Ferris wheel.

Chapter 14
Working with Your Inner Artist: a few final words

FEEDBACK

Receiving and interpreting external feedback is one of the trickiest jobs of you the practical-self. It is your job to protect the artist-self from nasty surprises and rude shocks to its ego. When receiving feedback, pull on your most serious business persona. Your practical-self must become Donald Trump in his boardroom.

Here are our tips:

- No outsider access. Know for a fact that nothing can touch your artist-self unless you are silly enough to let it through.
- Become a translator. Your job as a practical-self is to interpret feedback and turn it into instruction for the artist-self, not to allow anyone else to communicate in there.
  - "Your hero is wish-washy." Your job is to translate that for your artist-self as: "What can we do to beef up this hero? We want him to kick serious butt!"
  - "The composition on this print is all strange, I keep looking over here." Translate to: "What can we do to draw the attention of the viewer over there where we want it?"
- Don't read your own reviews. Have someone, anyone, filter reviews for you and only show you the good ones. Sure as hell don't pay attention to the folks on Goodreads, Amazon, or wherever your art is ranked by Jane or John Generic.

- You are the captain of your own ship. Decide consciously and calmly what feedback you think has justification. Reject the rest. Not from ego, but from a place of knowledge and practice.
- Rejection is not about you and probably not about your art. There are dozens of reasons that your art was not accepted, sold, reviewed, won the prize, or whatever you were expecting. They just bought one similar to it, the gallery is closing but not telling anyone yet, they're so overstretched / overstocked that they can't take another, you sent it to the wrong market (jazz to a rock and roll label, romance to a science fiction publisher…) or the key decision maker just isn't a fan of your type of art. Oh, it could be the quality of your work, but that's way down the list. So don't take rejection personally. Take it as an indicator that you still have more marketing work to do in order to get your art in front of the right person. Just move on.

TACKLING THE MESS

How do you wrap your hands around all this?!

You can't swallow the elephant whole. We've just distilled twenty or more years of learning into these brief pages.

Pick up one piece today and try it on for size. Does it fit? Remember our early instructions, discard that which doesn't work. Perhaps apply the tool of three weekly goals and make one of your goals to try the techniques you liked from this book, one by one, over time.

We've also tried to open new avenues of thinking about your art. Perhaps Albert Einstein said it best:

> *There was this huge world out there,*
> *independent of us human beings*
> *and standing before us like a great,*
> *eternal riddle,*
> *at least partly accessible to our*
> *inspection and thought.*
> *The contemplation of that world*
> *beckoned like a liberation.*

HOLD YOURSELF GENTLY

This is perhaps the best words of advice we can give you. Be kind to yourself, your integrated practical-artist-self. You will make mistakes, screw up deadlines, accidentally delete days or weeks of work with no backup. It happens to all of us! Trust me, no matter what creative screwup you discover, we can point to someone who has done worse.

The very best thing you can do at that moment is shrug, laugh, and remember the old Japanese proverb:

Fall down 7 times. Get up 8.

BROTHER'S EXPERIENCE
When I started working on this project, I thought I had bitten off the impossible task. It had started as a one-hour talk to seventy professional Project Managers at the Portland Chapter of Project Management International. In that form, it was using writing as a framework to illustrate project management methodologies in an atypical application.

Shortly after that, the task became much more complicated. I was asked to condense years of study into an hour-and-a-half talk for the Portland Chapter of the Romance Writers of America aimed not at Project Management but rather at the craft and business of being a writer. I am thankful for the kindness and great questions those fine fellow romance authors offered. I subsequently reworked various sections of this talk to audiences of a hundred or more.

A year later, I was asked to present the concepts, which had grown with time, in just one hour. It was to be a high-level lecture to an Advanced Master Class of thirty-five professional authors who among the group had produced well over five hundred books, many on the bestseller lists, others headed there. In the weeks it took me to build that presentation, it began to take on a form and structure that had previously eluded me.

In building this volume, I can only hope that you have learned even a small portion of what I have learned in writing it and also that you have enjoyed the experience even half as much as I did.

Thank you for listening. If I have helped in any way, that is a mitzvah.

SISTER'S EXPERIENCE

When my brother proposed collaborating on this idea, I wanted to refuse. The idea of exposing my artist-self to any sort of a formalized written structure just seemed weird and frankly impossible. It has turned out to be an interesting experience.

I hope that I haven't sounded peevish about any of the suggestions in this book. If I have at all it's likely to have come from the fact that I, like many of you, get a lot of structure, strategic goals, valued behaviors, advice about list-making at work. Part of the function of the studio is to give me "dreamtime," time to just get back into a more natural flow.

That said I'd like to point out that my brother is one of the most productive "makers" I know of. Personally I liked his index card idea a lot and am going to test that one out first. It's physical, it's visual, it is likely to fit me. There are quite a few other organizing principles and goals suggestions that I think are also great in this book.

If "goal" is a word that's too associated with outside work and opposed to your inner artist, consider the word "vision." I've had a good deal more success when I decide what I want, make it concrete, and work toward it (okay I know that makes it a goal but I don't call it that). I write it down, I think about it. I keep it simple.

I know that this kind of internal organization really really does matter. I know that one of the other big things too is to thank your friends and sponsors. Not only does it acknowledge achievement and help but very often new things open up after giving thanks.

Mom was right, a thank you letter goes a long way. My experience in the arts has convinced me that people are touched by the humanistic connections as long as they're authentic. Allowing some of that often-shy self to come out and make decisions and connections in a comfortable way has worked far better for me than forced networking.

Be prepared when your great opportunity comes.

YOUR EXPERIENCE

We'd love to hear your thoughts, experiences, suggestions, and anything else you'd like to say.

For further information on our art:

Matt –http://www.mlbuchman.com

Melitte –http://www.melittebuchman.com

e-mail –InnerArtist@buchmanbookworks.com

Thanks for taking the time to join us on the journey.

OTHER FINE BOOKS BY M.L. "MATT" BUCHAMN

Stragtegies for Success
Managing Your Inner Artist/Writer
Estate Planning for Authors

SF/F Titles
Nara
Monk's Maze
the Me and Elsie Chronicles

The Night Stalkers
MAIN FLIGHT
The Night Is Mine
I Own the Dawn
Wait Until Dark
Take Over at Midnight
Light Up the Night
Bring On the Dusk
By Break of Day
WHITE HOUSE HOLIDAY
Daniel's Christmas
Frank's Independence Day
Peter's Christmas
Zachary's Christmas

OTHER FINE BOOKS BY M.L. "MATT" BUCHAMN

Roy's Independence Day
Damien's Christmas
AND THE NAVY
Christmas at Steel Beach
Christmas at Peleliu Cove
5E
Target of the Heart
Target Lock on Love
Target of Mine

Delta Force
Target Engaged
Heart Strike

Dead Chef Thrillers
Swap Out!
One Chef!
Two Chef!

Firehawks
MAIN FLIGHT
Pure Heat
Full Blaze

OTHER FINE BOOKS BY M.L. "MATT" BUCHAMN

Hot Point
Flash of Fire
Wild Fire
SMOKEJUMPERS
Wildfire at Dawn
Wildfire at Larch Creek
Wildfire on the Skagit

Deities Anonymous
Cookbook from Hell: Reheated
Saviors 101

Angelo's Hearth
Where Dreams are Born
Where Dreams Reside
Maria's Christmas Table
Where Dreams Unfold
Where Dreams Are Written

Eagle Cove
Return to Eagle Cove
Recipe for Eagle Cove
Longing for Eagle Cove

OTHER FINE BOOKS BY M.L. "MATT" BUCHAMN

Keepsake for Eagle Cove

www.ingramcontent.com/pod-product-compliance
Lightning Source LLC
Chambersburg PA
CBHW030053100526
44591CB00008B/132